Continue your adventure in history with three FREE historical novels from James Rada, Jr.

Visit *jamesrada.com / newsletter-email*
and enter your email
to receive your FREE novels.

CRITICAL ACCLAIM FOR
THE WORKS OF JAMES RADA, JR.

The Last to Fall

"Authors Jim Rada and Richard Fulton have done an outstanding job of researching and chronicling this little-known story of those Marines in 1922, marking it as a significant moment in Marine Corps history."

> - *GySgt. Thomas Williams*
> *Executive Director*
> *U.S. Marine Corps Historical Company*

"Original, unique, profusely illustrated throughout, exceptionally well researched, informed, informative, and a bit iconoclastic, "The Last to Fall: The 1922 March, Battles, & Deaths of U.S. Marines at Gettysburg" will prove to be of enormous interest to military buffs and historians."

> - *Small Press Bookwatch*

Saving Shallmar

"But Saving Shallmar's Christmas story is a tale of compassion and charity, and the will to help fellow human beings not only survive, but also be ready to spring into action when a new opportunity presents itself. Bittersweet yet heartwarming, Saving Shallmar is a wonderful Christmas season story for readers of all ages and backgrounds, highly recommended."

> - *Small Press Bookwatch*

Battlefield Angels

"Rada describes women religious who selflessly performed life-saving work in often miserable conditions and thereby gained the admiration and respect of countless contemporaries. In so doing, Rada offers an appealing narrative and an entry point into the wealth of sources kept by the sisters."

> - *Catholic News Service*

Between Rail and River

"The book is an enjoyable, clean family read, with characters young and old for a broad-based appeal to both teens and adults. Between Rail and River also provides a unique, regional appeal, as it teaches about a particular group of people, ordinary working 'canawlers' in a story that goes beyond the usual coverage of life during the Civil War."

- *Historical Fiction Review*

Canawlers

"A powerful, thoughtful and fascinating historical novel, Canawlers documents author James Rada, Jr. as a writer of considerable and deftly expressed storytelling talent."

- *Midwest Book Review*

"James Rada, of Cumberland, has written a historical novel for high-schoolers and adults, which relates the adventures, hardships and ultimate tragedy of a family of boaters on the C&O Canal. ... The tale moves quickly and should hold the attention of readers looking for an imaginative adventure set on the canal at a critical time in history."

- *Along the Towpath*

October Mourning

"This is a very good, and very easy to read, novel about a famous, yet unknown, bit of 20th Century American history. While reading this book, in your mind, replace all mentions of 'Spanish Flu' with 'bird flu.' Hmmm."

- *Reviewer's Bookwatch*

SECRETS OF
FREDERICK COUNTY

Little-Known Stories & Hidden History
From Maryland's Largest County

Other non-fiction books by James Rada, Jr.

Non-Fiction
- Battlefield Angels: The Daughters of Charity Work as Civil War Nurses
- Beyond the Battlefield: Stories from Gettysburg's Rich History
- Clay Soldiers: One Marine's Story of War, Art, & Atomic Energy
- Echoes of War Drums: The Civil War in Mountain Maryland
- How to Make a Living Freelance Writing
- The Last to Fall: The 1922 March, Battles & Deaths of U.S. Marines at Gettysburg
- Looking Back: True Stories of Mountain Maryland
- Looking Back II: More True Stories of Mountain Maryland
- No North, No South: The Grand Reunion at the 50th Anniversary of the Battle of Gettysburg
- Saving Shallmar: Christmas Spirit in a Coal Town

Secrets Series
- Secrets of Allegany County: Little-Known Stories & Hidden History From Mountain Maryland
- Secrets of Catoctin Mountain: Little-Known Stories & Hidden History Along Catoctin Mountain
- Secrets of Deep Creek Lake: Little-Known Stories & Hidden History In and Around Maryland's Largest Lake
- Secrets of Franklin County: Little-Known Stories & Hidden History on Pennsylvania's State Line
- Secrets of Garrett County: Little-Known Stories & Hidden History of Maryland's Westernmost County
- Secrets of the C&O Canal: Little-Known Stories & Hidden History Along the Potomac River
- Secrets of the Gettysburg Battlefield: Little-Known Stories & Hidden History from the Gettysburg Battlefield
- Secrets of the Washington County: Little-Known Stories & Hidden History Where Western Maryland Starts

For historical fiction by James Rada, Jr., visit jamesrada.com.

SECRETS OF FREDERICK COUNTY

Little-Known Stories & Hidden History
From Maryland's Largest County

by
James Rada, Jr.

LEGACY
PUBLISHING
A division of AIM Publishing Group

SECRETS OF FREDERICK COUNTY: LITTLE-KNOWN STORIES &
HIDDEN HISTORY FROM MARYLAND'S LARGEST COUNTY
Published by Legacy Publishing, a division of AIM Publishing Group.
Gettysburg, Pennsylvania.

ISBN 979-8-9903256-2-3

This is a collection primarily of articles that have previously appeared in
Frederick Magazine, Catoctin History, The Frederick News-Post, The
Thurmont Dispatch, The Emmitsburg Dispatch, and The Catoctin Banner.
In some cases where additional information is available the stories have
been updated.

Cover design by Grace Eyler.

LEGACY
PUBLISHING
315 Oak Lane • Gettysburg, Pennsylvania 17325

CONTENTS

Frederick County, Maryland

While Frederick County, Maryland, is still the largest county by land area in the state, it used to be even larger. It comprised all of Western Maryland and then some.

The county was formed in 1748 from Prince George's County and Baltimore County. It is not known for certain who the county's namesake was.

It is generally believed to be Frederick Calvert, the sixth and last Lord Baltimore, who was the Proprietor of Maryland from 1751 until his death in 1771 in Naples, Italy. Maryland was formed as a proprietary colony, and proprietors were essentially colonial governors. As a former Proprietor of Maryland and a member of the founding family of Maryland, this makes for a strong case in his favor as Lord Baltimore as the namesake. He did not become Proprietor of Maryland until three years after Frederick County was formed, however.

It has also been suggested that the county might have been named after Frederick, Prince of Wales. Frederick was the eldest son and heir apparent to King George II. However, he did not have a good relationship with his parents, King George and Queen Caroline. He never became king because he died before his father. Frederick's eldest son became King George III when King George II died.

Frederick, Prince of Wales, has a number of places named in his honor, including Fredericksburg, Virginia; Prince Frederick, Maryland; Fort Frederick, Maine; Fort Frederick, South Carolina; Fort Frederick, New York; and Fort Frederica, Georgia; Fort Frederick, Maryland; Point

Frederick, Ontario; Fort Frederick, Ontario; and Fort Frederick, New Brunswick.

Daniel Dulany the Elder also used the prince's name, not so much in a strategic way, but to attract Germans to Frederick Town, which he founded.

Frederick Calvert
Sixth Lord Baltimore

"Daniel Dulany's desire to attract Germans to settle his town (and later county) most certainly lends credence to 'Frederick' being a highly attractive name choice. Prince Frederick Louis had remained a favorite among his kinsman, and in 1745 was still heir to the throne once his father passed. Dulany was in the position to have a double victory once King Frederick became a reality," Chris Haugh wrote is his article, "Frederick, Maryland's

4

Forgotten Frederick."

While the State of Maryland lists Frederick Calvert as the namesake of the county, it also notes that he is "probably" the person after whom the county is named.

Frederick, Prince of Wales

The definitive answer appears to have been lost to history.

For the next 18 years after its founding, Frederick County made up present-day Montgomery, Washington, Allegany, and Frederick counties. In 1776, Montgomery County formed from Frederick's southern portion and Washington County formed from the western end of Frederick County. Then, in 1837, an eastern portion of Frederick County combined with part of Baltimore County to form Carroll County. The remaining 667 square miles form modern Frederick County.

Frederick County has a rich history as the home to Founding Fathers, Civil War battlefields, and the presidential retreat.

Today, it continues to straddle two worlds with growing

urban centers, in particular, the City of Frederick, and strong agricultural areas.

And between the two are where the secrets lie.

INTERESTING
PEOPLE

Finding the Lost President

W hile it's not so much a secret that John Hanson, a resident of Frederick Town, was the actual first President of the United States, what was literally a secret for decades was where his final resting place was located.

Most people consider George Washington the first President of the United States, and he was. He was elected the first president of the country governed by the U.S. Constitution in 1789.

However, between the signing of the Declaration of Independence in 1776 and ratification of the Constitution in 1788, our brand new country was governed by the Articles of Confederation. It was the colonists' first attempt at creating a national government that would govern over the states in a fair manner.

Once in place, the Articles of Confederation showed its shortcomings, such as creating a weak federal government that interfered with states' abilities to conduct foreign diplomacy. This led to the Constitutional Conventions and the creation of the Constitution.

The head of the government under the Articles of Confederation was also called the president, although he was actually the president of Congress, which was largely a ceremonial position, according to the National Archives. However, he was the person who had to sign the official documents for the country.

On November 15, 1781, a small notice ran in The (Annapolis) Maryland Gazette that read, "On Monday last, pursuant to the articles of confederation, a sufficient number of delegates for the States having met, the United States in Congress assembled proceeded to the choice of president for the ensuing year, and the ballots being taken, the honourable JOHN Hanson was elected."

John Hanson, first President of the United States. Courtesy of Wikimedia Commons.

Although Hanson was the first leader of the United States, his office was so weak that this announcement wasn't even major news. It ran at the bottom of page 2 of the newspaper.

Hanson was born in Port Tobacco Parish, Charles County, in 1715, but he moved to Frederick Town in 1769, to work as a deputy surveyor. He lived at a house near the intersection of Patrick and Court streets. In 1771, he also became the sheriff of Frederick County, according to the MD Two Fifty website. He chaired the Frederick County Committee of Observation and was also elected as the county treasurer.

He was a delegate to the Continental Congress from 1780 to 1782. It was during this time that he signed the Articles of Confederation as part of the Maryland congressional delegation. This led to his election to the office of president in November 1781.

"One week later he considered resigning from this position because of poor health, family responsibilities, and the 'irksome' qualities of the 'form and ceremonies' required as president," according to the MD Two Fifty website.

He was convinced to remain and serve out his term until November 4, 1782. During his time in office, a consular service was established, a post office department created, a national bank chartered, a uniform coinage system adopted, established Thanksgiving Day as the fourth Thursday in November, and made movement toward taking the first national census, according to the Architect of the Capitol.

Hanson died on November 15, 1783, at the age of 68, in Oxon Hill, Maryland.

And this is where the mystery begins.

Following Hanson's death, his body was interred in a crypt on his nephew, Thomas Hanson's Oxon Hill Manor. In 1808, the Addison Family created its cemetery just 400 feet from Hanson's crypt at Oxon Hill Manor. Two years later, the Addisons sold Oxon Hill Manor to the Berry Family, though they retained the rights to continue using the cemetery, according to johnhansonmemorial.org. The last known burial in the cemetery was made in 1871.

When Oxon Hill Manor went into receivership in 1878, the four bodies in the crypt were moved to the Addison family cemetery.

According to johnhansonmemorial.org, by the 1930s that reinterment was forgotten since it had been done privately, and Hanson's gravesite was unknown. For decades, Hanson remained the only American president whose final resting place was not known.

In 1985, according to johnhansonmemorial.org, a state survey located the crypt where Hanson had originally been buried. The survey noted it was intact and sealed. However, two years later, an archeological survey found the crypt empty.

Not knowing the bodies had been moved a century earlier, the initial belief was that the graves had been robbed and that John Hanson's body had disappeared.

Oddly, the crypt even disappeared. A 1993 photo of the property where the crypt should have been didn't show it.

Then, in 2017, all the remains from the Addison family cemetery were re-interred at St. John's Episcopal Church graveyard in Fort Washington, Maryland. This proved lucky because the Smithsonian Institution took the opportunity to do a forensics examination of the remains.

According to johnhansonmemorial.org, "[Peter] Michael's records of Smithsonian Institution 2017 forensics examination of 40 sets of remains from Addison Cemetery reveal a solitary unidentified elderly male who can only be John Hanson."

Further, Peter Michael and Mark Kennedy pooled their research on Hanson in 2024 and used a chain-of-title for the land records of Oxon Hill Manor to rediscover that Hanson had been re-interred to the Addison family cemetery in 1878.

The lost president had been found.

Today, a reconstruction of Hanson's house can still be found at 100 W. Patrick Street in Frederick. The original building had been listed on the National Register of Historic Places in 1971, but it was demolished in 1981. It was removed from the National Register of Historic Places and the reconstructed building was added.

A national memorial statue of Hanson stands outside of the courthouse on West Patrick Street.

The John Hanson National Memorial Statue in front of the Frederick County Courthouse. Courtesy of Wikimedia Commons.

Born a Slave, "Miss Ruthie" Became Living History

T o most people, Ruth Bowie, or "Miss Ruthie" as she was called, was just a friendly old lady with a warm sense of humor and a sweet tooth. What they didn't realize was that she was also a historical figure in Frederick County.

When Miss Ruthie died in 1955, she not only was the oldest person in Frederick County (anywhere from 105 to 110, depending on which account was used), she was also the last person in the county who had been born into slavery.

As old as...

No one made an official record of Ruth Brown's birth in the mid-19th century. The 1900 U.S. Census listed her as 40 years old, but by the 1920 census, she had aged 25 years.

"Nobody knows just how old Miss Ruthie is, least of all Miss Ruthie herself," Betty Sullivan wrote for The Frederick Post. Sullivan also noted that Ruth couldn't remember ever celebrating a birthday as a child.

She is believed to have been born on the Asbury Mullinix Farm in Montgomery County. However, Kay Mehl wrote in The (Baltimore) Sun Magazine in 1955 that Bowie was born elsewhere and "'just a toddler' when sometime before the war she was sold in Montgomery County to a family named Mullinix."

The Asbury Mullinix farm was located on Long Road off

14

Long Corner Road in Damascus. It was part of a small community called Mullinix Mill, but the buildings burned down long ago.

Ruth's parents were Wesley and Letha Brown.

Marilyn Veek, a research assistant at the Maryland Room in the C. Burr Artz Library, found the description of Asbury Mullinix's slaves in the 1850 and 1860 Slave Schedules. In these documents, slaves are listed by their description and owner rather than their name.

In 1850, Mullinix owned seven slaves, including females aged 28 years, 14 years, and 6 months. On the 1860 Slave Schedule, he owned nine slaves, including three females ages 11, 8, and 4.

"Since Ruth Bowie's obituary indicates that she may have been born between 1845 and 1850, it is theoretically possible that she could be the female slave aged 6 months in the 1850 Slave Schedule and the female slave aged 11 years in 1860," Veek wrote in an e-mail.

Veek also noted that Ruth's parents were listed in the regular 1860 census, which implies that they have may have been freed. That census also only lists them as having a single daughter, 1-year-old, named Ann.

"One possibility is that they had been freed by Asbury Mullinix, but that their older children had not, and remained as slaves on his farm," Veek wrote.

Bob Hilton, a great-great-grandson of Asbury Mullinix, suggested another possibility. The Browns may have been freed slaves who still worked for the Mullinixes.

"Asbury had a habit of freeing slaves at 30 years old," Hilton said. "They just never left the place."

This had to do with Mullinix's view of slaves. Hilton has a set of letters exchanged between Mullinix and a doctor in Virginia. In the letters, the doctor argues that slaves aren't even human while Mullinix says that, yes, they are human, but they are like children who need to be taken care of.

The Browns were still living in the same area in the 1870 U.S. Census. They are listed as having three daughters, Ellen, Mary and Susan. Ruth Brown doesn't appear in the 1870 census associated with them.

Miss Ruthie in an old newspaper photo.

Slave life

Letha Brown was a house servant and cook for the Mullinixes while Wesley was a field hand.

"Well she remembers the days of her slavery when custom permitted owners to wield the whip 'for the least little thing' and little Ruthie often felt the sting of the switch," Sullivan wrote.

However, Ruth's experience with this came from her interactions with Asbury's wife, Elizabeth Mullinix, whom she called "Ol' Missy."

Hilton said he had no doubt that Ol' Missy beat Ruth. "She treated everybody like that not just Ruth," Hilton said. "Family stories say she was a crazy woman."

For the most part, Ruth worked in the main house. She was brought up to be a house servant like her mother. She would wash and iron clothes, clean the house, and take care of the Mullinix children.

"Often she would sit on a three-legged stool, crooning to the baby while her mistress in long hooped skirts worked a spinning wheel across the room," Mehl wrote.

During Ruth's childhood, the Mullinix farm switched from growing tobacco to general farming. This meant that fewer slaves were needed to handle the workload.

"Tobacco had blighted the land and general farming wasn't as labor intensive as tobacco farming," Hilton said.

So Mullinix reduced the number of slaves he owned. The ones he freed and who chose to remain on the farm help with the raising of corn, wheat, and cattle.

The Civil War

In her old age, Ruth still had memories of soldiers riding along the country roads in Montgomery County during the War Between the States. Some of the soldiers would camp near the Mullinix farm, steal horses, or just generally frighten people.

Nearly 100 years after the fact, Ruth still remembered the day soldiers broke into the main house looking for food. She heard them coming and hid behind a sugar barrel.

One of the soldiers found her and yelled, "I'm hungry!"

"They's meat in the pot an' bread in the box," Ruth whispered in fright.

The soldiers took the meat and bread and left without causing any more problems except that the family went hungry that night.

Though Ruth could remember the incident past her 100th birthday, whether the soldiers had been Union or Confederate escaped her.

Another day that Ruth never forgot was April 14, 1865, the day Abraham Lincoln was assassinated.

What's less certain is whether she attended the Gettysburg Address two years prior.

"Now she doesn't know, but young friends say years ago she used to talk about that great day in Pennsylvania and they're prone to believe that she was there," Sullivan wrote.

Ruth stayed with the Mullinixes until she married Charles Bowie in 1880. He had fought in the war on the Union side. After the war ended, he had returned to Frederick County to work for Dr. T. E. R. Miller until he fell off a wagon, injuring his right arm so badly that it had to be amputated.

Growing old

By the turn of the 20th century, the Bowies were listed as living in log home along Lewistown Pike in Lewistown, which is where they would call home for their rest of their lives. They had had four children together, but none of them lived to adulthood and then Ruth had to deal with the loss of her husband in 1920.

The (Frederick) News reported that Ruth was over 100 in 1946. The newspaper ran a short article noting that Ruth's doctor had decided that she was too old to continue living alone. Her sight and hearing were still considered normal, but she had hurt her hip shortly after she had turned 100 a year earlier. The doctor wasn't sure that she could continue caring for herself.

"The first hundred years aren't the hardest. It's after the first hundred years that things begin to get tough," she told the newspaper.

The Frederick Emergency Hospital, which is now the Montevue Assisted Living Center, became Ruth's new home. She became a fixture there sitting in her low, broad-armed chair and relating her quickly fading memories to her friends, who would come to visit her.

"For a woman who has had only one day's schooling in her life, she is remarkably discriminating in her choice of words. There was almost a wink in her smile when she related that she had not gone back to school after her teacher had whipped her on the first day because she was so 'full of devilishness,'" Mehl wrote.

When her friends visited, they would often bring her treats of chicken, sugar cakes and peppermint candies, which were Ruth's favorite foods.

"I like peppermint candy best," Ruth told The (Baltimore) Sun Magazine.

According to Diane Grove, administrator at Montevue Assisted Living Center, Ruth was discharged from the emergency hospital on May 22, 1955, at the age of 107.

When Ruth died later that year on November 23, she was the oldest resident of Frederick County. She had also been readmitted to Montevue because of her deteriorating health. The Rev. Charles Corbett officiated at her funeral when she was buried at Creagerstown Lutheran Church Cemetery.

"Every life is important and every story has its place in history but it's what you do with that life that's important," said Dwight Palmer, president of the Frederick County NAACP.

Though Bowie was not a civil rights icon, she represented the goals of the civil rights movement. She had risen from slavery to make a life for herself. She was well loved in the community by people of all colors. Despite the fact that she had no family to care for her, friends had visited Ruth frequently during her time at Montevue. Also, at a time when segregation still existed, Ruth's pallbearers were all white men who considered themselves her friends.

Patsy Cline: A Frederick County Music Creation

T
he legendary country singer, Patsy Cline, was born in Frederick County.

Before you scream, no, she was born in Winchester, Va., hear me out.

Virginia Patterson Hensley was born in Winchester in 1932, but it wasn't until she started performing in Brunswick and married Gerald Cline from Frederick that Patsy Cline was born.

Virginia Hensley

Virginia, or Ginny as she was called, was born in Winchester, but her family relocated to many cities throughout the state as her blacksmith father, Samuel Hensley, found work. However, the family eventually settled back in Winchester, and this is where Ginny called her hometown.

A talented performer, even as a young child, Ginny contracted rheumatic fever and a throat infection when she was 13 years old. She credited this disease with changing her singing voice and leading to her signature booming voice.

"I developed a terrible throat infection and my heart even stopped beating," she said in a 1957 interview. "The doctor put me in an oxygen tent. You might say, it was my return to the living after several days that launched me as a singer. The fever affected my throat, and when I recovered I had this booming voice like Kate Smith's."

Her interest in singing increased, and she began performing with a church choir.

Her father left the family in 1947, which was probably for the best. After Cline's death, it came out that Samuel Hensley had sexually abused his daughter. However, with her father gone and not supporting the family, Ginny had to drop out of John Handley High School in Winchester to help support her family.

She continued singing and even earned an audition with Grand Ole Opry at age 15. Nothing came of it, though, and she returned to Winchester to perform in the region.

Virginia Hensley aka Patsy Cline.

Gerald Cline

Ginny first started singing in Brunswick on September 27, 1952. "She had a contract to play the local Moose club with a performer named Bill Peer and his band," said Jim Castle with the Brunswick Heritage Museum. She would be a regular performer on Saturday nights with Bill Peer and the Melody Boys for three years.

She was a popular performer, always trying to please the audience. Douglas Gomery wrote in *Patsy Cline: The Making of an Icon* that one Brunswick "old timer" told him, "We'd shout out a request and she'd say 'I never heard that one yet, but I'll learn it!'"

Patsy Cline performing at the Brunswick Moose Hall with Bill Peer. Photo courtesy of the Stewart Bell Jr. Archives at the Handley Regional Library in Winchester, Va.

Some sources say Ginny's relationship with Peer soon turned into a love affair, although Peer was married. The affair also didn't stop Ginny from pursuing other relationships besides the one with Peer.

"She actually met her future husband, Gerald, at the Moose Club," Castle said.

According to a timeline compiled by G. E. Hewitt and Ron McBride, Ginny met Gerald Cline at the Brunswick Moose Lodge on October 11, 1952. Although Gerald lived in Frederick, he had come to Brunswick for the performance. He was immediately taken with Ginny. During the band's first break, he asked her if she would join him for a drink. Not surprisingly, Peer hovered close by. Gerald charmed Ginny, and the two soon became an item.

In *Honky Tonk Angel, An Intimate Story of Patsy Cline,* Gerald's brother, Nevin, told biographer Ellis Nassour that the despite the Cline family owning a contracting and excavating company in Frederick, Gerald was only "Saturday night rich", meaning he had money after payday but spent it quickly on women and having fun. Nevin also had a poor view of his brother's work ethic.

"He never lifted a finger to help us," Nevin told Nassour. "Gerald was supposed to drive one of the trucks, but he'd only do it if he was forced. Dad finally gave up on him and, in the end, made him secretary of the company, but I don't know what he ever did even in that position. He was good at one thing, being a ladies' man."

At five feet eight inches tall and 220 pounds, Gerald was not considered a handsome man, but he was fun to be around and made his dates feel like they were the center of the universe. He had no trouble finding women. In fact, he had been married previously and had a son. He was also eight years older than 20-year-old Ginny.

"It might not have been love at first sight when Patsy saw me, but it was for me," Gerald said in *Honky Tonk Angel.*

Gerald doted on Ginny while they dated, buying both her

and her mother gifts. He would even drive to Winchester to pick up Ginny and drive her to work. Although she was still seeing Peer, Gerald and Ginny married in a small, private ceremony on March 7, 1953, in the Reformed United Church of Christ in Frederick.

The couple first lived in a home Gerald's father, Earl Cline, owned in the Linden Hills area.

Around this time, Peer encouraged Ginny to adopt a stage name that was catchier than Virginia Hensley. She used her married name and a variation on her middle name, Patterson.

And with that, Patsy Cline was born.

Patsy Cline

Although the Clines' marriage gave the world one of the greatest country singers, it seemed doomed from the start.

"All the Hensleys agreed that Gerald was a nice man who dearly loved Ginny, but she was less smitten because of his continual demands that she give up singing," Gomery wrote.

Patsy was also still carrying on her affair with Peer. Once, Gerald came home unexpectedly when Peer was with Patsy. According to Nassour, Peer wound up hiding under the bed until Gerald fell asleep, and he could sneak out.

Gerald still doted on his wife at the beginning of the marriage, even buying her a new Buick Roadmaster in her favorite colors (red and white), according to Gomery.

The Clines moved from Linden Hills to the second floor of 824 East Patrick Street. Later, they moved in with Cline's parents at 436 East Patrick to save money, and before they divorced, they lived in a trailer park west of Frederick.

Since Gerald was not too committed to the family business, he often traveled with Patsy as she performed in different venues. This soon grew old for Cline, or perhaps he wanted to separate his wife from Peer. "Gerald wanted Patsy home with his supper and slippers, waiting when he got there," Nassour wrote. "That wasn't Patsy. Their arguments were legend with the downstairs neighbors."

Patsy Cline performing at the Brunswick Moose Hall. Photo courtesy of the Stewart Bell Jr. Archives at the Handley Regional Library in Winchester, Va.

Gomery credits Gerald with helping his wife get her first record contract that she signed on September 30, 1954. In August, Gerald drove Patsy to compete in the Fourth Annual National Championship County Music Contest in Warrenton, Va. She sang "Faded Love" and won $100 as the best female vocalist. This got her a job offer from Connie B. Gay, the event sponsor, at his radio station WMAL-AM in Arlington, Va.

"At first she sang advertising jingles," Gomery wrote.

"What Connie B. Gay's connection did offer was a record contract with William McCall, owner of the 4-Star label, of Pasadena, California."

Other sources give Peer an even larger role in helping Patsy land the deal because he created a demo tape of Patsy singing and sent it to different record labels. He also signed as the witness on Patsy's Four Star Records contract.

The fighting and infidelity got to be too much, and Patsy left Gerald for good in March 1956. Their divorce was finalized a year later. Gerald blamed Patsy's mother and Peer for the breakup in his marriage.

Less than a month after the Clines' divorce was final, Patsy met Charlie Dick, the man who would become her second husband.

Patsy's big break came when she won Arthur Godfrey's Talent Scout program on January 21, 1957. She sang "Walkin' After Midnight" and won the competition that evening. Although Patsy had already recorded the song, it hadn't been released as a single. Decca Records rushed it into release, and it peaked at No. 2 on Billboard's Hot Country and Western Sides chart, and it also reached No. 12 on the Billboard's pop chart. Not only was Patsy a country star, she was also a pop star.

Surprise appearance

In 1958, Patsy, Roy Clark, and Jimmy Dean sang at the Brunswick Fire Hall for a special fundraising performance. The show raised money for 5-year-old Vicki Stair, who suffered burns over 45 percent of her body from an accident. Then-Brunswick Fire Chief Sonny Cannon put the benefit together. It was a hit and drew people from all over the area.

Brunswick resident Mary Jo Brown was in the audience. "She had a great voice," Mary Jo said. "She came out to sing during Jimmy Dean's break. No one knew beforehand that she was going to sing."

Mary Jo and her friends were excited about being able to attend the performance. "We couldn't see her at the Moose Lodge because they served alcohol," she said.

The performance stuck in Mary Jo's mind so much that she helped organize a 50th anniversary recreation of the concert in 2008.

Patsy Cline performing at the Brunswick Moose Hall. Photo courtesy of the Stewart Bell Jr. Archives at the Handley Regional Library in Winchester, Va.

"More than 350 paid $45 in advance or $50 at the door. This was a fundraiser for three nonprofits. The program included live music with a set of Patsy covers," wrote former Brunswick Mayor Carroll Jones in an e-mail. He was a friend of hers from childhood.

"I met Patsy in the fall of 1947 (she was 15, I was 13) when we rode the same school bus in Loudoun County, Virginia," he wrote.

By 1960, the Grand Ole Opry corrected its earlier mistake of rejecting Patsy, and she became a member. She soon became a hit maker with songs like "I Fall to Pieces," "She's Got You," and "Crazy."

On March 5, 1963, Patsy was flying home from a benefit show in Kansas with fellow performers Cowboy Copas, Hawkshaw Hawkins, and manager Randy Hughes. The plane hit rough weather and crashed, killing everyone aboard.

"When she was killed in that plane crash, the people of Brunswick lost a friend," Mary Jo said.

Carroll said many residents took a certain pride in Brunswick's role in Patsy's career. "Expressed in another way, many viewed her as a 'hometown girl'," he said.

Patsy Cline is now considered one of the greatest country singers of all time. Would Virginia Hensley have done as well? It's something we'll never know.

Some of Patsy Cline's Frederick County appearances and connections

From G.E. Hewitt and Ron McBride's "Patsy Cline Timeline":

1952
- Sept. 27: Ginny Hensley's debut in the Brunswick Moose Hall with Bill Peer and His Melody Boys.
- Oct. 11: Ginny met her future husband, Gerald Cline, at the Brunswick Moose Lodge.

1953
- Feb. 27: Applied for a marriage license in Frederick.
- Mar. 7: Married Gerald Cline in the Reformed United Church of Christ in Frederick.
- Jul. 20: Performed at the Family Drive-In in Frederick.

1954
- Jun. 22: Performed at Firemen's Carnival in Middletown with Bill Peer and his Melody Boys.

- Jun. 28: Performed at Firemen's Carnival in Woodsboro with Bill Peer and his Melody Boys.
- Nov. 20: Rehearsed with Bill Peer and his Melody Boys in Brunswick.
- Dec. 11: Rehearsed with Bill Peer and his Melody Boys in Brunswick.
- Dec. 31: The Clines and Peers rang in the new year at the Brunswick Moose Lodge.

1955
- May: Private session at WFMD studio with Bill Peer's Melody Boys in Frederick.
- Jul. 9: Performed at Brunswick Moose Lodge.
- Oct. 15: Final appearance with Bill Peer at Brunswick Moose Hall.

1956
- Jul. 13: Performed at Firemen's Park in Mount Airy with Ham 'n Scram and Buzz Busby.

1957
- Mar. 28: Gerald Cline granted Patsy a divorce
- Sept. 8: Patsy's 25th birthday celebration at the Brunswick Moose Lodge.

1958
- Mar. 5-8: Patsy was to perform during one of the four days the show ran, but canceled because of a booking in Hawaii.
- Summer: Performs at the Brunswick Fire Hall with Jimmy Dean.

1959
- Jun. 27: Performed at the Casablanca in Thurmont.
- July 1: Performed at the District Volunteer Fire Company Carnival in New Market.

The Founder of Boys Town Returns to the Town that Gave Him His Start

T he second of back-to-back Best Actor Oscars that the legendary Spencer Tracy won was for his role in the 1938 movie Boys Town. He played the role of Father Edward Flanagan, the Catholic priest who founded the pioneering boys' home in Nebraska. The home is credited for giving many disadvantaged youths a better life and helping them through their struggling childhood.

Flanagan was also a graduate of Mount St. Mary's College in Emmitsburg, and he also had some struggles while there.

During his first day on campus, a schoolmate pushed him into St. Anthony's Lake.

"I learned to swim because I had to," Flanagan told The Frederick Post in a 1945 interview. He later credited that experience and forced swimming lessons with allowing him to save his 75-year-old father from drowning on a fishing trip.

His second day on campus was just as noteworthy. "When a schoolmate challenged him to a fight in the gym, the youngster from Ireland proved himself a willing mixer. The battle lasted four hours," The Frederick Post reported.

His opponent spent the next week in bed. "I was in worse shape than he was and the only reason I didn't go to bed, too, was because I was new in this country and too green to know that I should have," Flanagan told the newspaper.

Luckily, most of his time at the Mount was not so exciting.

He applied himself to his studies and developed a focused concentration on his work that would help him later in life.

Fr. Edward Flanagan, class of 1906, visits the Mount in November 1945. Photo courtesy of Mount St. Mary's University.

Flanagan's biographers have noted that Flanagan enjoyed his time in Emmitsburg and his frequent visits to his alma mater bear this out. He sang with the glee club and chapel choir and was elected to the Sodality of the Blessed Virgin Mary. The (Frederick) News also noted in a 1982 article that Flanagan was considered the best handball player on campus.

When he graduated in 1906 as the youngest in his class, he was recognized for his distinguished study in Latin and Greek and for a speech called "The Gaelic Revival" during the college elocution contest.

His one regret, apparently, was that he didn't get into any trouble. According to The (Frederick) News, it was a tradition at the time a boy had to get in trouble with the administration at least once during his time at the Mount to be considered a true "Mountaineer."

"Perhaps I should have misbehaved a little," Flanagan was quoted in one of his biographies.

He was granted a Master's Degree from the Mount in 1911 while he was working in Austria. It was during this time overseas in Austria and Rome when he was also ordained a priest.

When he returned to the U.S. in 1913, he worked in Omaha as the assistant pastor at St. Patrick's Catholic Church and the proprietor of the Workingmen's Hotel, which was temporary housing for vagrants. Seeing these men, Flanagan began wondering if they would have led different lives if they had been helped as boys.

This led to his idea of opening a home for boys in 1917. The Boys' Industrial Home began with only five boys. It was more than just an orphanage, it was a home for boys that also used new parenting methods to raise and educate the boys so that they would be productive adults. As it grew in size, it was renamed Boys Town.

While the Spencer Tracy film was great PR for the organization, the film actually caused cutback in donations. "Viewers apparently made the judgement that if Boys Town could survive all the crises contained in the film, Flanagan and his troops might then withstand anything else that might happen," according to The (Frederick) News.

In 1938, Mount St. Mary's awarded Flanagan an honorary Doctor of Laws in recognition of his work at Boys Town.

Flanagan died in 1948 at the age of 52.

"To have actually lived Flanagan is perhaps too much the perpetrator of the happy ending, too strong the personification of the American dream come true," The (Frederick) News noted.

The Zimmerman Family and Their Flying Machines

M an has long wanted to fly like the birds. Icarus and wings from Greek mythology are one of the early examples of this. The problem was that even as man learned how to leave the earth behind, he couldn't find a way to control his flight. He was at the mercy of the winds, much like the old sailing ships.

Then the Wright Brothers made the first controlled and sustained flight on a powered, heavier-than-air craft on December 17, 1903. The world changed.

One of the Wright Brothers' contemporaries was Dr. Charles Zimmerman of Braddock Heights, Md. He had been fascinated with flight for about as long as the Wrights had, and Anne Hooper in *Braddock Heights: a glance backwards* wrote that the Wrights and Zimmerman had corresponded.

Born in Charlestown, W.Va., in 1852, Zimmerman had moved to Frederick, Md., in 1893 after leaving his successful practice in New York because "it proved too onerous for his health," according to The (Frederick) News.

Soon after that, his experiments in creating a flying machine began. Small advertisements appeared in the newspapers offering a toy flying machines and tailless kites for 10 cents (about $6 in today's dollars).

These toys also served as the models for his own experiments in manned flight. In 1902, the newspaper began reporting that Zimmerman was close to creating an "aeroplane." His goal was to have something that he could enter in the

1904 St. Louis World's Fair.

A $100,000 prize (about $5.5 million in today's dollars) was being offered to the person who could navigate an airship over a 15-mile planned course in an hour. It was a sizable prize that attracted a lot of inventors.

A volunteer glides through the air using one of the wings of Charles Zimmerman's flying machine. Scanned from The Frederick News.

By 1902, the Zimmermans were spending their summers in Braddock Heights where the doctor continued his experiments. It seemed that he was close and expected his flying machine to carry passengers. In an interview in The (Frederick) News, he said that he had made all of his friends and family parachutes "in case any should be timid enough to want to back out."

He noted that he had faced a lot of doubters, but he believed that man would be able to fly someday.

"We believe the aeroplane idea will come to the front and take the lead, soaring and flying over, under and around any balloon that was ever made, regardless of wind or weather, for the harder the wind blows the less work has the aeroplane man. He can go into the eye of the then, like an ice boat, or across or with the wind," Zimmerman told the newspaper.

The flying machine invented by Charles Zimmerman's sons gets a test flight. Scanned from The Frederick News.

The June 7, 1902, issue of the newspaper showed one of his experiments. One of the wings (which was 35 feet by 3 feet) of his craft was tethered to a tree and a seat attached to it. The picture showed the wind lifting a boy into the air. Essentially, it was not much different from a parachute caught in an updraft.

Zimmerman's design called for two wings the size of the one in the picture.

"The operator grasps the inner end of the wing arm with his hands, with his feet on the pedals on wheels, and flaps their wings up and down to get propulsion. The wheels enable the machine to run along on the ground until a speed of about 20 miles an hour is attained," The (Frederick) News reported.

The problem, admitted Zimmerman, was reaching the required 20 miles per hour. "I have not yet struck the happy combination of mechanical adjustment of parts of the machine to the highest ideal development of muscular energy of the human frame," he said.

The answer continued to elude him, and by September 1903, he had begun to doubt himself and the idea of flight, at least in the near future. He told a reporter that he questioned whether anyone would be able to win the $100,000 in St. Louis. It was just a few months later that the Wright Brothers made their historic flight, and Zimmerman's enthusiasm was rekindled.

He was correct about the World's Fair prize, though. No one captured the award in St. Louis the following year. However, Roy Knabenshue did pilot the "California Arrow," a powered balloon, on a 37-minute flight 2,000 feet above the fairgrounds. It was the most successful of several airships and balloons that tried for the prize.

T. S. Baldwin built the "California Arrow." From pictures, it resembles what would eventually become a dirigible. In fact, Knabenshue would go on to become the country's first dirigible pilot and build the first passenger dirigible in America. The "California Arrow" only carried one person, though. Knabenshue stood on a triangular frame below an oblong balloon. He turned the airship by shifting his weight to one side or the other.

Zimmerman's health soon deteriorated, and he died from tuberculosis on March 5, 1908, at the age of 56. He left behind a wife and four children. His sons, Charles and Harry, soon took up their father's passion with a goal of making his dream a reality as a way to honor their father.

On September 5, 1908, the Zimmerman Brothers demonstrated their own flying machine, which was based on their father's designs. They took the machine up on National Pike as it crossed the top of Catoctin Mountain and started down toward Middletown.

A young boy named Russell Lowe, who weighed 110 pounds, was strapped into the seat of the craft, which was pointed into the wind.

"The wind raised the machine from the ground, and sustained it while it was propelled a distance of about 25 feet, when it was pulled to the ground," The (Frederick) News reported.

The flight was repeated a few hours later, with Robert McCutcheon as the pilot.

While the Zimmermans' airplane test was successful, the newspaper noted, "While the circular plane intended to maintain the equilibrium of the machine could not be revolved fast enough to demonstrate its worth, the inventors were much pleased with the demonstration of the sustaining power of the planes of the machine."

The flight must have ignited an interest in flying in McCutcheon. Hooper noted in her book that McCutcheon, with the help of the Keller Brothers, would go on to build a bi-plane glider that was able to fly.

How a Lincoln Conspirator Came to Call Emmitsburg Home

J ohn Surratt Jr. hated life in Emmitsburg, Md., but then he hated life in America. Maybe that was why he tried to kidnap the President of the United States.

Surratt was born April 13, 1844, in Washington, D.C., the youngest of John and Mary Surratt's five children. When the Civil War broke out, Surratt was attending St. Charles College near Baltimore. His father died in 1862 while Surratt was home, and he did not return to complete his schooling. Instead, he was appointed U.S. Postmaster of Surrattsville, Md., but he also became a postmaster of sorts for the Confederacy. He carried letters and troop information to Confederate boats on the Potomac River during the war.

"We had a regular established line from Washington to the Potomac, and I being the only unmarried man on the route, I had most of the hard riding to do. I devised various ways to carry the dispatches - sometimes in the heel of my boots, sometimes between the planks of the buggy," Surratt said in an 1870 speech.

Samuel Mudd introduced Surratt to John Wilkes Booth on December 23, 1864, in Washington. Surratt willingly joined in Booth's conspiracy to abduct President Abraham Lincoln by stopping his carriage while it was en route to a destination.

"To our great disappointment, however, the President was not there but one of the government officials - Mr.

[Salmon P.] Chase, if I mistake not. We did not disturb him, as we wanted a bigger chase than he could have afforded us. It was certainly a bitter disappointment, but yet I think a most fortunate one for us. It was our last attempt," Surratt said.

John Wilkes Booth assassinates President Abraham Lincoln at Ford's Theater. Courtesy of the Library of Congress.

On the night Booth and some of Surratt's other co-conspirators attempted a triple assassination of Lincoln, the vice president and the secretary of state, Surratt said he was in Elmira, N.Y., spying for the Confederacy. However, it was believed initially that Surratt attempted to assassinate the secretary of state. Surratt found himself a wanted man with a $25,000 bounty on his head.

Surratt fled to Canada. "A parish priest, Father Charles Boucher, gave sanctuary to the former Catholic seminarian, and Surratt remained there in hiding from mid-April through the trial, conviction, sentencing, and hanging of his mother. He followed the trial by reading the papers and through secret correspondence with friends in Washington. In all that time, from the end of April to the first week of July, Surratt made no effort to save his mother from the gallows. Later, he blamed his friends for failing to inform him about the true peril that Mary Surratt faced," James Swanson wrote in *Manhunt: The 12-Day Chase for Lincoln's Killer.*

Mary Surratt was arrested, tried and hanged with three other conspirators—George Atzerodt, Lewis Paine, and David Herold.

From Canada, Surratt fled to England in September 1865 and then onto Rome, where he joined the Papal Zouaves, the army of the Papal States. On a trip to Egypt in 1866, Surratt was identified as a Lincoln conspirator and arrested.

John Surratt's mother, Mary, was among the four conspirators tried and hanged for their roles in Lincoln's assassination. Photo courtesy of the Library of Congress.

One of the first wanted posters issued after the assassination lists a $25,000 reward for Surratt's capture as an accomplice of John Wilkes Booth. Photo courtesy of the Library of Congress.

He was returned to the United States where he stood trial in a civilian court that began on June 10, 1867. After testimony from 170 witnesses, the trial ended two months later with a hung jury. The government eventually dropped the charges and Surratt was freed in the summer of 1868.

"John Surratt was a free man. His mother was dead, he had been exposed as a leader in a plot to kidnap President Lincoln, and he had earned the reputation of a coward who had abandoned his mother to die. But at least he was alive. If he had been captured in 1865 and tried by military tribunal, he certainly would have been convicted, and would likely have been executed," Swanson wrote.

Surratt sought to turn his experiences into a career on the lecture circuit. He readily admitted a part in the kidnapping but denied involvement in the assassination. When his speaking tour was canceled because of public outrage, Surratt took up teaching. Following a stint as a teacher at a school in Rockville, Md., he used his Catholic connections to secure a position in Emmitsburg.

One source puts Surratt in Emmitsburg as early as 1870, teaching at St. Joseph's School, which was identified as being held in the old fire hall opposite St. Joseph's Church.

"He rattled his classes and resorted to physical punishment to maintain discipline. On older boys, some of them twenty or twenty-one, he used his fists. The younger boys John would beat with a paddle after he had stretched them over a special punishment desk which he had designed," according to a 1938 letter by Frederick Welty.

Sandra Walia with the Surratt House Museum's James O. Hall Research Center doubts this could have been Surratt because his students nicknamed the man in Welty's letter "Old Bear" and Surratt would have only been about 27 years old at the time, barely older than the oldest boys he taught.

Another account, which comes directly from Surratt, said

he left his teaching position in Rockville in 1873 and took a job as principal at St. Vincent's Academy in Emmitsburg with 60 students. This was probably St. Vincent's Hall, which was built in 1857 as a combination school and literary and social center next to St. Joseph's Church. The Daughters of Charity took over the teaching there in 1878, so the 1873 date for Surratt's tenure would have been right.

John Surratt in his uniform as a Papal Zouave in Rome. Photo courtesy of the Library of Congress.

During his time at St. Vincent's Academy, Surratt wrote to Father Jolivet, who had sheltered him in England when he had fled Canada after Lincoln's assassination. "My greatest desire, Father Jolivet is to leave this abominable country and go to Europe there to spend the balance of my days in peace and quiet," Surratt wrote.

At the time Surratt wrote the letter, he had been married 11 months to Mary Victorine Hunter, a second cousin of Francis Scott Key. He was also the father of a newborn son. Shortly after that, the Surratts moved to Baltimore, where Surratt took a job at the Baltimore Steam Packet Company.

When he died of pneumonia on April 21, 1916, at age 72, he was the last surviving member of the Lincoln conspiracy and the only one known to have called Emmitsburg home.

AMERICA'S PASTIME

Frederick Baseball Showed Some Hustle in the Blue Ridge League

O n Thursday morning, May 27, 1915, H.A. Albaugh showed his love of baseball in two ways. He drove 42 miles over stone and hard-packed dirt roads from his home in Westminster to Frederick in order to see the Frederick Hustlers make their professional baseball debut. The drive took him about two hours and before leaving home, he made a bet with a friend that Frederick would win its opening day game. If the Hustlers lost, Albaugh promised that he would walk home.

It was a daring bet. The Hustlers were playing the Martinsburg Champs, who had been the league champs in the defunct Tri-City League the previous year. Albaugh and Frederick had chosen their champion, though, and the Hustlers didn't disappoint.

Professional baseball comes to Frederick

Though baseball came to Frederick County near the beginning of the 20th century, it wasn't played professionally in the county until 1915. Until that time, you could watch town teams compete against each other.

The semi-pro Sunset League formed in 1907 and included a team from Frederick. The league, which was named because its games were played from late afternoon until sunset, folded in 1911. Then, in 1914, the Frederick Hustlers became part of the Tri-City League with Hagerstown and Martinsburg, W.Va.

As the season was winding down, Charles Boyer, a former president of the South Atlantic League, moved back to the Hagerstown area. He watched the town teams playing against each other and saw that there was talent among the players that deserved to be rewarded.

Charles F. Goodell, a prominent Frederick doctor who served as vice president of the league and president of the Frederick team for a number of years. Photo courtesy of Arcadia Publishing.

He purchased the Hagerstown team and set to work forming a new baseball league that would soon be named the Blue Ridge League. Boyer wanted the league to be a professional league, which meant that it needed a minimum of six teams.

"The Frederick team had been called the Black Sox in the Tri-City League, but as the Blue Ridge League started, they had a very fast team so they became the Hustlers," said Mark Ziegler, who runs the website BlueRidgeLeague.org.

Boyer started with the three teams of the Tri-City League and was able to convince Chambersburg and Gettysburg in Pennsylvania to field teams. While the league certainly had enough teams to play the 1915 season, it was short the needed number to petition the National Commission (now the National Association of Professional Baseball Leagues) for professional status.

Then in March 1915, Hanover joined the league and the Blue Ridge League was granted Class D recognition—the lowest class of professional status in baseball.

"It was entry level baseball," said Robert Savitt, author of *The Blue Ridge League* and a Myersville resident. "Even though the players got paid, they still needed to have other jobs."

As the teams set about recruiting players, they had little to offer, despite the fact they were professional teams. Frederick lost the chance of having Ty Cobb's younger brother play for the Hustlers because the team had already reached its $500 a month salary cap, according to The Frederick Post.

Opening day

With the introduction of professional baseball to the region, towns caught baseball fever.

"Not a thing has been left undone to make the big day of the advent of Frederick into organized baseball one long to be remembered..." The Frederick Post reported on May 27, 1915, opening day for the season and the league.

The Frederick mayor and aldermen declared the day a

half holiday, and most businesses closed their doors in the afternoon so that both employees and customers could go out to Agricultural Field to watch the Hustlers play the Martinsburg Champs. While the Hustlers were the hometown favorites, the Champs had won the 1914 pennant in the Tri-City League.

The events of the day kicked off with a parade at 1:30 p.m. A marching band struck up "It's a Long Way to Tipperary" and started down Patrick Street. Frederick Police Chief George Hoffman riding a horse and leading most of the Frederick Police force walked in front of the band. The parade continued with 20 cars and six carriages carrying the players and other officials, including Mayor Lewis Fraley, Alderman Lloyd Culler, and Alderman Henry Abbott.

Valley ▲ Spirit

The Official Schedule of the Blue Ridge League, 1915

READ	AT CHAMBERSBURG	AT FREDERICK	AT HAGERSTOWN	AT HANOVER	AT GETTYSBURG	AT MARTINSBURG
CHAMBERSBURG	VALLEY	June 11, 12, 8 / July 21 July 5 p.m. / July 28, 29 / Aug. 20, 21, 8	May 28, 29, 8 / June 21, 22 / July 14, 15 / Aug. 1, 6	May 31 a.m., p.m. / June 30, July 1 / July 23, 24, 8 / Aug. 16, 17	June 4, 5, 8 / June 28, 29 / July 21, 22 / Aug. 13, 14, 8	June 16, 17 / July 9, 10, 8 / Aug. 2, 3 / Aug. 25, 26
FREDERICK	June 9, 10 / July 3, 8, 5 a.m. / July 26, 27 / Aug. 18, 19	SPIRIT	June 4, 5, 8 / June 28, 29 / July 21, 22 / Aug. 13, 14, 8	June 14, 15 / July 7, 8 / July 26, 31, 8 / Aug. 23, 24	May 31 a.m. / June 16, 17 / July 9, 10, 8 / Aug. 2, 3–25, 26	May 28, 29, 8 / June 21, 22 / Aug. 6, 7, 8
HAGERSTOWN	May 27 / June 18, 19, 8 / July 6 / July 12, 13, 8 / Aug. 5, 7, 8	June 7, 8 / June 30, July 1 / July 23, 24, 8 / Aug. 16, 17	LEADS	June 16, 17 / July 9, 10, 8 / Aug. 2, 3 / Aug. 25, 26	June 14, 15 / July 20, 21, 8 / July 7, 8 / Aug. 23, 24	May 31 p.m. / June 3 / June 25, 26, 8 / July 19, 20 / Aug. 11, 12
HANOVER	June 7, 8 / June 23, 24 / July 16, 17, 8 / Aug. 9, 10	June 2, 3 / June 25, 26, 8 / July 19, 20 / Aug. 11, 12	June 11, 12, 8 / July 5 a.m., p.m. / July 28, 29 / Aug. 20, 21	IN	May 27, 29 / June 21, 22 / July 6 / July 14, 15 / Aug. 6, 7, 8	June 9, 10 / July 2, 3, 8 / July 26, 27 / Aug. 18, 19
GETTYSBURG	June 2, 3 / June 25, 26 / July 19, 20 / Aug. 11, 12	May 31 p.m. / June 17 / June 23, 24 / July 16, 17, 8 / Aug. 9, 10	June 9, 10 / July 2, 3, 8 / July 26, 27 / Aug. 1, 5	May 27, 29, 8 / June 18, 19, 8 / July 12, 13 / Aug. 4, 5	ALL	June 11, 12, 8 / July 5 a.m. p.m. / July 28, 29 / Aug. 20, 21, 8
MARTINSBURG	June 14, 15 / July 7, 8 / July 30, 31, 8 / Aug. 23, 24	May 27 / June 18, 19 / July 7 / July 12, 13 / Aug. 4, 5	May 31 a.m. / June 2 / June 23, 24 / July 16, 17, 8 / Aug. 9, 10	June 4, 5, 8 / June 28, 29 / July 21, 22 / Aug. 13, 14, 8	June 7, 8 / June 30, July 1 / July 16, 17	SPORTS

The 1915 schedule for the Blue Ridge League. Photo courtesy of Arcadia Publishing.

The parade proceeded to the cemetery and then traveled to the fountain on North Market Street, down Market Street to the town square and out to Agricultural Park. The Fairgrounds Board had built the field in 1903 at the southwest corner of the fairgrounds.

An estimated 3,000 fans turned out to see the 3:30 p.m. game. Frederick won with a final score of 14-3.

"The game was a slaughter from the time Frederick began scoring in the second round until the last Martinsburg player was out in the ninth and by the time the sixth had arrived the fans had lost interest," reported The Frederick Post.

It seemed that the Hustlers were on fire. From the opening day victory, they went on to win 17 of their first 20 games of the season.

Playing the big boys

As the season progressed, the Hustlers looked like they were unstoppable. However, on August 31, 1915, they were stopped quickly and decisively. The new professional baseball league had caught the attention of major league coaches like Jack Dunn and Connie Mack. They were on the lookout for new talent.

Mack had already stolen away one of the Hustlers named Lew "Cy" Malone.

"Cy Malone was an infielder for the Hustlers before Mack took him up to the majors," says Ziegler.

On August 31, Malone, Mack, and the Athletics came to Frederick to play the Hustlers. Turnout at Agricultural Field was back to its opening day level.

Frederick took an early lead in the game, but "A fusillade of extra-base hits in the ninth inning of yesterday's great game at Agricultural Park, enabled the Philadelphia Athletics to carry off a victory," according to The (Frederick) Daily News. The final score was 7-3.

The newspaper noted that Malone played well and "looked like a big leaguer from every angle."

Champions

By mid-August, the Hustlers had clinched the first pennant for the Blue Ridge League with six scheduled games left.

"They have obtained such a lead in the last month that it will not be necessary to play off the several postponed and tie games," The (Frederick) Daily News reported.

The Hustlers finished the season with a record of 53-23-1. The team also finished the season with the top hitter and pitcher in the league. Bobbie Orrison from Brunswick was an outfielder with a .341 batting average. Bill King of Jefferson was the pitcher with 17 wins.

Team photo of the 1915 Frederick Hustlers who won the pennant that year with a 53-23-1 record. Photo courtesy of Arcadia Publishing.

It had also been a financially successful season. The Frederick Post noted the following year that, "The fans were joyous, we had a winning club, the pitchers and the best hitter was also a member of the Hustlers. Yes, we were proud of our team and at the end of the season when the receipts were totaled it was found as already expected that the gate receipts of the Frederick club were far in advance of any other."

For Hustlers' catcher, Poke Whalen, the championship was even more important. He not only won a pennant, he won his wife. Nellie Wallet of Baltimore had promised to marry him if the Hustlers won the championship.

"This cheered Poke on and after the pennant was declared Frederick's property, Poke went to Baltimore and had some minister to declare that Miss Wallet now belonged to him," The Frederick Post reported.

Recapturing the magic

However, as the Hustlers tried to maintain their championship title the following season, they faltered.

Though Martinsburg's 1915 team had been the Champs, the Hustlers took the name for 1916, which seemed to set off a slew of name changes for the teams. The new name was no help. The Frederick Champs finished the season at 46-51. They took it as a bad sign and changed back to the Hustlers for 1917. However, Frederick wouldn't produce another championship team until 1921.

Big league buyout

Though the Major League teams recruited players from the Blue Ridge League, the teams remained independent. As the Blue Ridge League teams struggled financially, some dropped out of the league and others had to be added in order to maintain professional status.

In the late-1920s, the teams began agreeing to Major League ownership. Not only would the Major League team financially support the small Blue Ridge League teams, but they would also lend the prestige of their names to the smaller teams.

"The Blue Ridge League was the pioneer in the formation

of the farm system," Savitt said.

In 1929, the Cleveland Indians purchased the Hustlers, and the team changed its name to the Warriors, which was a better match with the parent team. The Indians had already plucked a Hustler from Frederick (Ray Gardner) years earlier and were hoping to develop more players in the future. The Indians even came to Frederick to play an exhibition game with the Warriors in June 1929.

"Having the Major League teams play exhibition games really generated fan interest," said Savitt.

Though the Blue Ridge League was on the lowest rung of professional baseball, it had a lasting impact on baseball in addition to introducing the farm system to the sport. The league also pioneered playing night games under bright lights and playing games on Sunday. The latter actually led to players being arrested for violating Blue Laws.

The end of the league

Despite the support of Major League ownership, the Blue Ridge League teams continued to struggle.

"With the stock market crash in 1929, a lot of Major League team owners lost money and could no longer support the Blue Ridge teams and the league never came back from that," Ziegler said.

The longest-running Class D baseball league ended its run on February 10, 1930.

A few attempts were made to revive the league in the 1930s and 1940s, but these leagues lasted only a few seasons and were never more than semi-pro.

The Blue Ridge League's legacy is not only the lasting changes that it introduced to baseball but also the many Major League players who got their professional start in the league. This includes Baseball Hall of Fame pitcher Lefty Grove who played with Martinsburg in 1920, outfielder Hack

Wilson who played with Martinsburg 1921-1922 and umpire Bill McGowan, who was with the league in 1917.

Clyde "Pooch" Barnhart, an early star in the Blue Ridge League, went on to play with Pittsburgh Pirates. Photo courtesy of the Library of Congress.

Frederick players who made it to the majors

Savitt said that he could count at least 100 Major League players who played for some time in the Blue Ridge League. Some of the ones from Frederick's teams include:

- Clyde Barnhart (1915) played with the Pirates 1920-1928.

- Lew Malone (1915) played with the Athletics and Robins 1915-1919.
- Bill Lamar (1915) played with the Athletics, Yankees, Red Sox and Robins 1917-1927.
- Chick Fullis (1924-1926) played with the Giants, Phillies and Cardinals 1928-1936.
- Rollie Hemsley (1925-1927) played with the Browns, Indians, Pirates, Yankees and Cubs 1928-1947.
- Ray Gardner (1920, 1922) played with the Indians 1929-1930.
- Jimmie DeShong (1928) palyed with the Senators, Yankees and Athletics 1932-1939.
- Joe Vosmik (1929) played with the Indians, Red Sox, Browns, Dodgers and Senators 1930-1944.
- Milt Galatzer (1930) played with the Indians and Reds 1933-1939.

The cities and teams of the Blue Ridge League

City	Team	Years
Chambersburg, Pa.	Maroons	1915-1917, 1920-1928
	Young Yanks	1929-1930
Cumberland, Md.	Colts	1917-1918
Frederick, Md.	Hustlers	1915, 1917, 1920-1928
	Champs	1916
	Warriors	1929-1930
Gettysburg, Pa.	Patriots	1915
	Ponies	1916-1917
Hagerstown, Md.	Blues	1915
	Terriers	1916-1918, 1922-1923
	Champs	1920-1921

	Hubs	1924-1930
Hanover, Pa.	Hornets	1915
	Raiders	1916-1917,
		1920-1929
Martinsburg, W.Va.	Champs	1915.
	Blue Sox	1916-1917,
		1922-1929
	Mountaineers	1920-1921
Piedmont, W.Va./	Drybugs	1918
Westernport, Md.		
Waynesboro, Pa.	Red Birds	1920,
		1928-1930
	Villagers	1921-1927

The Return of the King: The Babe Returns to Where He was Discovered

Word got around quickly that the Babe was back. The home run king of the American League had returned. Those who heard came to see him; some even took the trolley from Frederick to Thurmont and then switched to the Emmitsburg Railroad to make the rest of the journey to Emmitsburg. So when George Herman Ruth walked onto Echo Field at Mount St. Mary's College on May 7, 1921, a crowd was there to greet him.

The Babe discovered

The crowd was far larger than the one that had greeted him when he made his first appearance on the field in 1913.

At that time, Ruth was a young man of 18 years who was playing baseball with the team from St. Mary's Industrial School for Boys of Baltimore. The school was a reformatory and an orphanage. Ruth had been there since he was seven years old because his parents couldn't care for him.

Brother Matthias Boutlier, the Head of Discipline at St. Mary's Industrial School, introduced Ruth to the game of baseball, which he quickly took to. The team made the trip to Mount St. Mary's in 1913 to play a commencement day game against the Mount St. Mary's freshman baseball team as an opener to the alumni game that featured college alumni playing against the varsity team.

Babe Ruth. Courtesy of Wikimedia Commons.

The odds looked good for the alumni to win in 1913. They had Joe Engel, a pitcher for the Washington Senators, on the mound for them. He was able to play in the game since Sunday baseball wasn't allowed in Washington D.C. at the time and so he was off work.

The Babe comes to the plate. Photo courtesy of Mount St. Mary's University.

Engel had once been something special in his own right. When he had attended the Mount, he had lettered in track, baseball, basketball, and football. He also had pitched a perfect game while on the Mount baseball team. He pitched in the Major League from 1912 until 1920. When he was sent to the Minor League, Engel showed himself to be an excellent scout. He eventually became known as one of the greatest scouts and baseball promoter in the history of the game.

It could be argued that his talent first began to show itself in Engel in 1913. He was among the crowd who watched Ruth, who stood 6 foot 2 inches tall and weighed 170 pounds, strike out 18 of the 20 batters he faced.

"The St. Mary's pitcher caught Engel's eye, partly because of his fastball and partly because of his haircut. Ruth—he was the pitcher, of course—no longer wore his hair cropped short but instead was wearing it in the most mature hair style, that he, Engel, had ever seen on a school kid," Henry Thomas wrote in *Walter Johnson: Baseball's Big Train*. The haircut apparently was tightly clipped on the sides and "roached," or waved over his forehead. According to Thomas, it was "in the mode highly favored by bartenders and other cool cats of the day."

Engel said later of his first impression of Ruth, "He really could wheel that ball in there, and remember, I was used to seeing Walter Johnson throw. This kid was a great natural pitcher. He had everything."

Once the game had ended, Ruth cleaned himself up and joined the band to play the bass drum.

That evening on a train to Baltimore, Engel ran into Jack Dunn, the owner and manager of the Baltimore Orioles, which was a Minor League team that had no connection to the current Major League team with the same name. Engel knew Dunn professionally, and the two began to talk during the ride. When Dunn heard that Engel had been playing in his alma mater's alumni game, he asked if anyone on the college's team showed promise. Engel began talking about the young pitcher he had seen who could also play the drums.

"He's got real stuff," Engel told Dunn.

It was the first time Ruth's name was mentioned professionally, according to Tom Meany a writer who has written extensively about Babe Ruth.

Dunn made a note of the name, but he didn't immediately act on it. That came later when another person with a keen eye for baseball praised Ruth's ability.

The Babe gets a hit. Photo courtesy of Mount St. Mary's University.

"Then Dunn heard the same name from Brother Gilbert when he went to scout a possible pitcher at St. Joseph's. Brother Gilbert, wanting to keep his own player in school and pitching for St. Joseph's, began to extol the natural talent of a kid named Ruth over at St. Mary's. Dunn decided it was time to see for himself," wrote Wilborn Hampton in *Babe Ruth: A Twentieth-Century Life.*

Dunn went to St. Mary's Industrial School and watched Ruth pitch during a workout for half an hour and signed him to a contract for $250 a month on February 14, 1914.

George becomes Babe Ruth

By July, Ruth had made the jump to the Boston Red Sox to play in the Major League. He got his first victory pitching during his major league debut on July 11. He was sent back to the Minor League for a while and returned as a starter the following year. That season, his record was 18-8 and his batting average was .315. The Red Sox won that year's World Series and though Ruth played in it, he grounded out during his only time at bat.

By 1918, the Red Sox began to recognize Ruth's ability as a hitter. They began using him less as a pitcher and more as a hitter. That year, he led the American League in home runs, and the following year, he would set his first single-season home run record (29 home runs).

Ruth was sold to the New York Yankees in December 1919. During the 1920 season, Ruth hit 54 home runs with a .376 batting average, again setting records. His .847 slugging average would stand for more than 80 years.

This was the legend who returned to Mount St. Mary's. Discovered as a teenage pitcher there, he was now returning as the home run king.

The king returns

It was big news for Frederick County. Although The Frederick Post didn't routinely report on Emmitsburg news, it included a paragraph in its May 7, 1921, edition noting: "'Babe' Ruth, the home run king of the American League, spent last night at Mt. St. Mary's College. He passed through Frederick by auto about 8:30 o'clock yesterday evening. He will return to Frederick early this morning, making the return trip by automobile. He will pass through Frederick again between 8 and 8:30 o'clock."

Babe Ruth with Monsignor Benjamin Bradley.
Photo courtesy of Mount. St. Mary's University.

When Ruth had arrived at Mount St. Mary's College on Friday evening, he visited the faculty and met them. Then he visited a study hall to meet with students there and talk with them. It was there that the students convinced him to spend the night and give a demonstration of the talent that had made him a legend the next morning.

The good-natured Ruth relented, and word spread quickly that Ruth would be giving a hitting demonstration the next morning. And so, when Ruth stepped onto Echo Field the next morning, a crowd had gathered to see the man who was on his way to becoming a baseball icon.

"Time after time mighty shouts went up as the Terror of Twirlers sent the white pellet first over the tennis courts in right field and then over the bank in left. For nearly an hour, the King of Swat stood up to the plate and golfed the horsehide to all corners of the lot. He slammed them anywhere and everywhere. Slow ones, fast ones, it made no difference to the 'Bam,' he hit them all right on the old nose," The Mountaineer, Mount St. Mary's newspaper, reported.

Mike Gibbons, director of the Babe Ruth Museum, said, "He hit monstrous flies and let people catch them. He also let the pitcher strike him out, which the crowd loved."

Ruth stopped only because he needed to get on the road to be elsewhere, but he was besieged by fans who wanted a picture with him or signed balls and bats and "one guy presented a tattoo needle to stamp a little remembrance on for keeps," according to The Mountaineer.

Ruth left Emmitsburg and drove to Washington, where he played in a game against the Senators where he hit his eighth home run of the season.

The 1921 baseball season was a good year for Ruth. He hit 59 home runs, batted .378 and had a slugging average of .846 and led the Yankees to their first league championship.

The Major League Pitcher Who Disappeared from Emmitsburg

M any a young boy picks up a bat, walks to the plate and dreams of slugging his way into immortality. Tolbert "Percy" Dalton was such a boy, and he did manage to find his own type of immortality. Not because he is forever remembered as one of baseball's greats, but because he is one of the few major league players whose death date was unknown, and if not for some dedicated researchers, it may have remained unknown.

Besides being a baseball player, Dalton was a lay preacher for the Columbia Primitive Baptist Church in Burtonsville, Maryland.

"The church he was an elder in, to my knowledge, had other smaller worship locations in the state of Maryland. As an elder, we understand that he would make occasional appearances at Sunday services at the main church. He would speak to certain topics relevant to the beliefs the church had. He would also baptize new members," said Richard Bozzone with the Society for American Baseball Research (SABR).

On August 1, 1948, two deacons from the church visited Dalton's Emmitsburg home. Dalton had failed to show up for a church meeting on July 4.

Dalton had only lived in Emmitsburg for a year, having moved there from the Catonsville, Md., area to become editor of the Emmitsburg Chronicle when it restarted publication after a five-year hiatus during World War II. He and his wife lived with his wife's daughter and son-in-law, Lois and

George Heller.

The two deacons couldn't find Dalton. No one in his family knew what had happened to him.

Dalton, who went by the name of Jack during his baseball career, played seven seasons of professional baseball. He was an outfielder who started in the Minor League in Des Moines, Iowa. where he batted .208 in 1910. He was invited mid-year to join the Brooklyn Robins, predecessor to the Dodgers. He slumped and was sent to the Minor League team in Newark, N.J. He returned to the Robins in 1914 and then played for the Buffalo Blues in 1915 and Detroit Tigers in 1916. His best year was 1914 when he batted .319. The following year, his batting average was .293 with 28 stolen bases. He finished his career in 1916, playing most of the season for San Francisco in the minor leagues and eight games for Detroit.

However, by 1948, at 62 years old, his glory days were forgotten. Dalton was living in Emmitsburg with his second wife, Thelma Bradshaw.

Though Dalton was too old to steal bases, he possibly found one thing he could still steal. Ralph Harris, a former member, and editor of the Primitive Baptist Church newspaper, knew two of Dalton's sisters (now deceased). He asked them what happened to their brother.

"Their response was that he had absconded with the subscription funds for the church paper. Although Cary did not have firsthand knowledge of the theft, the story was confirmed by several of the church leadership when he became editor," Bozzone said.

Dalton happens to be one of the very few 20th century Major League players for whom death information is not known.

"There are 15 20th century players for whom we do not have death details, but Dalton is, by far, the most well-known of the players," Bozzone said.

Bozzone has been assisted in his search for Dalton by a SABR member, Al Quimby. What has made the task so difficult is that not even the family of Jack Dalton has information on what happened to him.

No missing person report appears to have ever been filed with the Maryland State Police. No articles about his death have ever turned up. He simply vanished.

Tolbert "Percy" Dalton

SABR member Bill Haber of Brooklyn, New York, also worked on the Dalton case. Though now deceased, Haber's research over 20 years has corrected errors in more than 200 professional baseball players' biographies. Haber tracked some of Dalton's relatives to Emmitsburg in 1978. He was told that Dalton had seemingly fallen off the face of the earth and never made contact with any of his relatives after he left Emmitsburg. He did not even show up for his brother's funeral in 1954.

Dalton was born July 3, 1885, in Henderson, Tenn. He had three sisters, Lura, Lena, and Lola and one brother named Pleasie.

Following Dalton's baseball career, SABR determined that in 1921 and 1922, he was a salesman living in Baltimore. In 1930, he was residing in Elkridge, Md. By 1940, he was living at Catonsville at 2 North Prospect St. In April 1942, his World War II registration cards lists him as a clerk in the Finance Office of the U.S. Army's Third Corps headquarters in Baltimore. After the war, he became involved with the Primitive Baptist Church and moved to Emmitsburg.

This was all that was known about Dalton for decades until Quimby came across Dalton's death certificate in Pittsburgh. The document stated that Dalton died of a heart ailment in Allegheny General Hospital on February 17, 1950. He was 64 years old. The certificate was discovered in 2012 when Pennsylvania allowed access to death records before 1961. The Social Security number confirmed that it was the same Tolbert Dalton who had disappeared from Emmitsburg.

What happened during the two years that he was missing and why he left are still unknown. One interesting point from the death certificate is that it stated Dalton was unmarried. This is incorrect. He was still legally married to Thelma Dalton at the time of his death. She died in 1966 in Royersford, Penn., which is across the state from Pittsburgh.

While there are still unanswered questions about Dalton, at least the mystery of his disappearance has been solved.

CALLED TO
SERVE

The Marines Take Frederick

E arly in the morning of Monday, June 19, 1922, more than 5,000 Marines—more than a quarter of the Corps—at the Marine Camp in Quantico marched on-to waiting barges supplied by the U.S. Navy. Four Navy tug boats towed the barges up the Potomac River toward Washington, D.C. Meanwhile, tanks and trucks hauling artillery pieces rolled out along the Richmond Road headed for the same destination.

The Marines were marching to save the Corps. Despite the Marines' valiant service in World War I, officials were considering disbanding the Marine Corps.

Maj. Gen. John A. Lejeune, Commandant of the Marine Corps, understood that his Marines needed to fight for survival in the political arena just as hard as they fought on the battlefield. He devised a campaign to raise public awareness about the value of the Marine Corps.

One of the ways he did this was instead of going to obscure places to conduct war games and train, he went to iconic places and put the Marines out in front of the public. At the time, the national military parks, such as Gettysburg, were still under control of the U.S. War Department, which meant the Marines could use the parks as a training ground. Lejeune chose to do just that with a series of annual training exercises, which commenced in 1921 with a re-enactment of the Battle of the Wilderness.

The 1922 march to Gettysburg not only involved thousands of Marines, but The (Baltimore) Sun noted, "The 5,000 men are carrying the equipment of a complete division of nearly 20,000. In the machine-gun outfits especially the personnel is skeletonized, while the material is complete. Companies of 88 men are carrying ammunition, range finders and other technical gear for companies of about 140."

The Marines en route to Gettysburg. Photo courtesy of U.S. Marine Corps Historical Society.

The march

The Marines spent their first night at East Potomac Park, south of the Washington Monument. Once they had fully set up camp on June 19, they marched past the White House and were reviewed by President Warren G. Harding and other dignitaries.

"Observers declared that this is the first time that troops have passed in review through the White House grounds since the Civil War," the Marine Corps Gazette reported.

It took a half an hour for the Marines to pass as the 134-piece combined Marine bands played music.

On June 20, the Marines marched to Bethesda, Md. The

following day they marched to Gaithersburg where they spent two nights. On June 23, they arrived in Ridgeville, Md., near Mt. Airy.

Marines encamped at the Frederick Fairgrounds in 1922. Photo courtesy of U.S. Marine Corps Historical Society.

Frederick

From Ridgeville, the Marines marched along the National Road to the Frederick Fairgrounds. The first Marines began arriving in Frederick at 9 a.m. on June 24, but the bulk of the group arrived around noon. By then, streetcars were carrying signs hanging along their sides announcing that the Marines had arrived at the fairgrounds. They were greeted with flags hanging from windows and thousands of people lining the road into Frederick.

"The old Frederick fair grounds, scene of famous gatherings each fall of people from all over the State to see horse races, prize pigs, pumpkins and side show freaks, is today a city of pup tents and motortrucks, with radio towers rising into the air at one side, smoke curling up from scores of field kitchens and band music floating down toward the city from leatherneck bands. Hundreds of automobiles journeyed out to see the sight," The (Baltimore) Sun reported.

Once the Marines were encamped, Frederick Mayor Lloyd C. Culler led a delegation out to the fairgrounds to greet them. Besides Culler, the delegation included Lorenzo Mullinix, president of Frederick Board of Aldermen; James H. Gambrill, Jr., Frederick Rotary Club president; Col. D. J. Markey on behalf of the Maryland governor and National Guard; Holmes D. Baker, president of the Frederick Chamber of Commerce; Albert S. Brown representing the Sons of the American Revolution; Rev. William Storm, vice-commander of the Maryland Department of the American Legion; Grayson H. Staley, president of the Frederick Kiwanis Club; David C. Winebrenner; and Charles C. Carty.

Culler urged Gen. Smedley Butler, who commanded the Marine expedition, to stay through Sunday, but Butler insisted there was a schedule that had to be kept. However, the general did invite any Civil War veterans in Frederick to be special guests of the Marines at Gettysburg. Butler attended a chamber of commerce dinner in Braddock Heights to the west of the city that evening as their guest of honor.

After the Marines had settled into camp Saturday afternoon, many of them watched the baseball game between the Frederick Hustlers and the Hanover Raiders, which was played on a field right next to the fairgrounds.

Leaving Frederick

Some Fredericktonians got up as early as 5 a.m. to line the streets, waiting to see the Marines march out of town on June 25.

"Gray-hair veterans and the silvery-haired women who had cheered the troops when they came through Maryland to save the North in the days from '61 to '65 watched with sparkling eyes and a far-away reminiscent gaze as they conjured up the scenes of long ago," reported The Washington Post.

Marines march down N. Market Street in Frederick on June 24, 1922. Photo courtesy of U.S. Marine Corps Historical Society.

The Marines marched into the city along East Patrick Street and then headed out of town by going north on Market Street.

"All along the road the Marines have been welcomed by admiring country people who cheer them on and invited them to 'hurry up and come back again and next time stay longer,'" The Frederick Post reported.

As the Marines neared the city limits, there had initially been a plan for a Barbara Fritchie re-enactor to wave to the

Marines as if they were Union troops in pursuit of Confederates. According to The (Baltimore) Sun, this didn't happen because Fritchie was considered a controversial topic in the town.

"Though her name is a household word in every Northern household, and millions of Americans know Barbara Frietchie (sic) and her flag defied the Confederate troops, about half of the people of Frederick never mention her name and scoff angrily whenever it comes up," according to The (Baltimore) Sun.

The woman was already in place at the window, but officials squelched the plan at the last minute.

Marines entering Thurmont on June 25, 1922. Photo courtesy of Thurmontimages.com.

Thurmont

The Marines reached Thurmont around 1:45 p.m.

"Everyone from the small boy to the aged veteran was up and out to await and see the soldiers. Sunday School and church attendance suffered severely, and no doubt the few who did attend wished they were out on the street. Many persons remained in town, preferring to miss their dinners rather than miss seeing this great military outfit arrive. Every porch along the State Road was crowded with people watching the passing trucks," The Catoctin Clarion reported.

Marine Camp Haines near Thurmont in 1922. Note the movie screen in the foreground used to show footage filmed while the Marines were marching during the previous day. Photo courtesy of Thurmontimages.com.

The Marines ran into a slight snag as they passed north along Church Street. The Western Maryland Railway passed over the road about three blocks north of the downtown square, and the trucks carrying the tanks didn't have enough clearance for to pass under the bridge. Heavy timbers had to be placed on the back of the trucks to allow the tanks to be unloaded. The trucks and tanks then rolled under the bridge separately. On the other side, the tanks were loaded onto the trucks again.

The final night of the march was spent on Hooker Lewis's farm just north of Thurmont.

Several Civil War veterans greet the Marines as they march through the center of Emmitsburg. Photo courtesy of the Town of Emmitsburg.

Hamilton crash

Capt. George Hamilton, in command of a squadron of fighters providing "scout duty" while escorting the Marine infantry, along with GySgt. George Martin, were flying a DH-4B fighter as they left their encampment at Thurmont shortly after noon on July 26 and proceeded north.

His De Havilland was at the rear of a formation of four planes serving as air scouts for the Marines marching from Thurmont to Gettysburg. Nothing amiss among the planes of the squadron was noticed until the flights began to approach the landing site at Camp Harding. Two of the planes in the escort landed safely in a designated portion of the fields near the intersection of Long Lane and Emmitsburg Road.

Then Hamilton and Martin's plane suddenly went into a nose dive from about 3,000 feet up. It then became a tailspin. The plane crashed on the William Johns farm around 1:05 p.m., near what is presently the intersection of Johns Avenue and Culp Street in the Colt Park development. The (Gettysburg) Star and Sentinel further stated the impact occurred within 50 feet of tents and equestrian equipment belonging to the Lew Dufour Carnival, which had set-up along Steinwehr Avenue.

Hamilton died at the scene, and Martin died a short time later at Warner Hospital.

Dismantling of the wreckage of a Vought VE-01 that suffered a hard landing in the Wheatfield at Gettysburg on the same day as the Hamilton-Martin crash. Photo courtesy of Leatherneck Magazine.

The accident is believed to have been due to the difference in the reading of the altimeter, by which fliers estimate their distance from the ground at Quantico and Gettysburg. Quantico is on sea level, while Gettysburg is 600 feet above sea level. Consequently, when the altimeter reads 1,000 feet at the latter place, the actual distance is only 400 feet.

Hamilton and Martin were regarded as having been killed in the line-of-duty in the service of their country, and the deaths of the two Marines are presently the only known military line-of-duty deaths that have occurred on the Gettysburg battlefield since 1863.

Marines begin to fall as the battle to capture the Codori house and farmstead gets underway. Photo courtesy of the Marine Corps Archives & Special Collections.

At Gettysburg

Camp was set up on the Codori Farm and just north of the North Carolina Monument and near the McMillan farmhouse near the farm and park boundary. The ultimate size of the encampment was reported by various newspapers to have been from 65 to 100 acres. GySgt. Thomas E. Williams, director of the United States Marine Corps Historical Company, stated that 100 acres is probably closer to the actual size of the encampment.

Due to the planned stay of President Harding and his wife, Florence, in the camp for a night, it was decided to build a "Canvas White House" for the president and his entourage. The final structure was an 18-room tent that had running water, electricity, and porcelain bathtubs for six bathrooms.

The main reason the Marines marched to Gettysburg was to train. They conducted a historical re-enactment of Pickett's Charge that 100,000 people turned out to see, including President Warren Harding.

However, the more dramatic re-enactment came after the crowds left. Then the Marines brought in their tanks, planes, and machine guns and fought Pickett's Charge as they would in 1922. It is the only time when the Union Air Force fought the Confederate Air Force for supremacy of the air.

Another stay in Frederick

After 10 days in Gettysburg, the Marines started marching back to Quantico on July 6. It was a retracing of the same route that they had taken from Quantico to Gettysburg, except for one difference. They decided to take the city up on its generous offer and spend two nights in Frederick and only a single night in Rockville.

The YMCA pool may have been the most popular site among the Marines. "At all hours the building was used by the soldiers who thoroughly enjoyed the facilities. The swimming pool and the showers were the greatest treat for the boys," reported The (Gettysburg) Star and Sentinel. An estimated 1,000 Marines made use of the pool.

The Marines received a distinguished visitor as President Harding, and his party stopped by on their way back from

Marion, Ohio. The Hardings' car stopped outside the camp, and the president and his wife stood in the road as the Expeditionary Force Marine Corps Band serenaded them.

That evening, the 134-member band (a combination of three bands) was again called on to perform. An estimated 5,000 people came into the city from Frederick County as well as other counties to hear the band play at the Court House Park at 7:30 p.m. It was the largest open-air concert ever held in the city of Frederick.

A few days later, the Marines were back in Quantico, having shown the world what they were capable of.

Secret Mission Transferred Command of the Union Army

O n Saturday night, June 27, 1863, a middle-aged man dressed in civilian clothing moved among the Union soldiers carousing in Frederick. The army was celebrating, but this man was solemn and determined.

"In spite of strict orders and guarded campsites, hundreds of men slipped into Frederick, 'made merry with the townsfolk, ate at hotel tables and drank at hotel bars, on the day and evening of the 27th.' Some say the Army of the Potomac consumed more liquor that night than any other night in the war. Quite a few obtained hangovers lasting until noon on Monday," wrote John Schildt in *Roads to Gettysburg*.

He added, "To make matters worse, it was Saturday night. For some reason, there was no provost marshal, and a carnival-like atmosphere prevailed. The streets of Frederick, and the roads leading to and from the town, were filled with drunken, boisterous soldiers. They were having a good time on Maryland whiskey."

When the civilian came across a sober soldier, he asked where Maj. Gen. George Meade could be found. Had the soldiers known they were addressing a colonel, they would have gone stone-cold sober. His name was Col. James Hardie of the War Department, but he was dressed as a civilian because he was on a secret mission for the United States government. He was under orders not to dress in uniform or tell anyone where he was going. He had been "given the necessary passes and money to buy his way to his destination if he encountered delay or opposition. If met by Stuart and the Confederate cavalry, he was to destroy his papers, endeavor to escape, and deliver his orders verbally," wrote Schildt.

The problem was that Hardie needed to find Meade to deliver his orders and complete his mission, but no one knew where the general was.

Finally, the colonel found a buggy driver who said he knew the whereabouts of Meade's headquarters. Hardie hired him and told him to hurry.

"His driver could make but slow progress through the parties of drinking soldiers and the wagon trains along the road. At times, Hardie had to dismount and beg officers to clear the way for him. This was done several times," Schildt wrote.

Hardie arrived at the Robert McGill farm in Arcadia in the early hours of June 28, 1863. It was on Buckeystown Road near Ballenger Creek, south of Frederick.

When he approached the general, a guard who didn't want to wake Meade barred Hardie from the general's tent. Hardie convinced the guard otherwise, entered the tent, and woke Meade.

The exchange between Hardie and Meade has been pieced together from a number of sources, most notably a letter from the general to his wife.

Once the general was awake and sitting up, Hardie said, "I've come to give you trouble."

Meade replied, "My conscience is clear. I have given offense to no man. I am prepared for your bad news." Though he could not imagine what the reason would be, he believed he was about to be arrested or relieved of command.

Hardie passed the general the sealed orders from the War Department. Meade opened them and read that he was now in command of the Army of the Potomac.

According to the letter to his wife, Meade shook his head. "No. This isn't right. The command should go to John Reynolds. It is an injustice to him."

"It is not my choice," Hardie replied.

"I don't even know the location of the commands of the Army of the Potomac, let alone the Confederates."

"The command is yours. We need to go let Gen. Hooker know."

"I can't go to Joe's tent and assume command. He is my superior. He should send for me."

"You no longer have a superior here. You are in command of the army."

Gen. George Meade. Photo courtesy of the Library of Congress.

Meade stood up, pulled back the tent flap and told the guard to prepare horses and an escort as quickly as possible, according to an eyewitness account that was later written down.

The group rode to Prospect Hall where Gen. Joseph Hooker had established his headquarters. When Hooker saw the group, he knew what was happening. Just the day before, he had asked to be relieved of the command he had held barely five months. Hardie delivered the news.

Meade, Hardie, Hooker, and Hooker's chief of staff, Daniel Butterfield, sat down to go over the maps and information Meade would need to command.

The formal change of command took place around noon on June 28, and Hooker left shortly thereafter.

Charles Coffin, a reporter on the scene, wrote, "Gen. Hooker bade farewell to the principal officers of the army on the afternoon of the 28th. They were drawn up in a line. He shook hands with each officer, laboring in vain to stifle his emotion. The tears rolled down his cheeks. The officers were deeply affected."

Meade approached his former commander. "The old and the new commanders shook hands, and talked in low tones. Then the wagon left and Meade walked into the headquarters tent. The burden of meeting and checking the enemy was now his," Schildt wrote.

It was now only three days before the Battle of Gettysburg and the turning point of the Civil War.

The Daughters of Charity were Battlefield Angels

N
o one would look at a Daughter of Charity and see the steel in their personalities that gave them the ability to venture where women rarely went in the 1860s. They ran schools, cared for the poor, and worked in hospitals.

The latter was frowned upon in the early 1800s. Nursing wasn't considered a suitable profession for women. Nursing in public hospitals was often done by other residents of the hospital or the poor. No formal training program existed.

That way of thinking began changing in the 1850s, though. The French Daughters of Charity had served as battlefield nurses caring for French soldiers during the Crimean War. Their service had been so exemplary that many people began looking at the American Daughters of Charity and wondering if they could do the same thing once the Civil War began.

As the United States broke apart, Daughters of Charity from Emmitsburg found themselves serving soldiers in both the Union and Confederacy.

Catholic sisters and war

Nearly 700 Catholic sisters from 22 orders provided some sort of service during the Civil War. The Daughters of Charity provided the largest number—around 300—to serve in the war.

"The country had only 600 trained nurses at the start of the Civil War. All were Catholic nuns. This is one of the best-kept secrets in our nation's history," Civil War chaplain Father William Barnaby Faherty once said.

Mother Ann Simeon led the Daughters of Charity during the Civil War. Courtesy of the Daughters of Charity.

Though the American Daughters of Charity had been in existence for 52 years by 1861, their mother organization in France has existed since 1617. Even before the Civil War, the Catholic sisters' future was tied to war. Not long after their founding, Founder Saint Vincent de Paul told the sisters, "Men go to war to kill one another, and you, sisters, you go to repair the harm they had have done... Men kill the body and very often the soul, and you go to restore life, or at least by your care to assist in preserving it."

The American Sisters of Charity started gaining experience in health care when they took over the administration of the Baltimore Infirmary in 1823. Their success with the care of the sick in the hospital led to them opening the first hospital west of the Mississippi River, St. Louis Mullanphy Hospital. They gained experience working with victims of violence, accidents, yellow fever and cholera. As their reputation grew as nurses, they opened additional hospitals and they were asked to assume the administration and nursing duties of others.

These varied experiences in dangerous surroundings became the training ground for what they would face in the war. In doing so, they also became the only source for trained nurses.

The Daughters of Charity had been providing nursing care to Confederate even before the outbreak of the war. Sister Regina Smith ran the Charity Hospital in Louisiana for the state and Daughters of Charity. In late March 1861, four prominent men in New Orleans approached her, and the Daughters of Charity to care for ill Confederate soldiers. This was about two months after Louisiana had seceded from the Union and a month after the Provisional Confederate Congress met and formed the military, and two weeks before Fort Sumter.

When war finally did break out, Daughters of Charity were in both the North and South in the Union states of New York, Massachusetts, Pennsylvania, Wisconsin, Michigan, Illinois, Maryland and California. In the Confederate States, they served in Louisiana, Mississippi, Alabama, Missouri and Virginia.

Dorothea Dix. Photo courtesy of the Library of Congress.

Dorothea Dix

Neither the Union nor the Confederacy was ready to care for those who survived the battles wounded and maimed at the start of the Civil War. They received volunteer help from various aid societies that formed after the start of the war and more-formal help with the appointment of Dorothea Dix as the superintendent of U.S. Army nurses.

However, Dix's authoritarian and biased management

style won her no friends. No woman under 30 years old need apply to serve in the government hospitals. All nurses were required to be plain-looking women. Their dresses had to be brown or black with no bows, no curls in their hair, no jewelry, and no hoop skirts. But for these requirements, there may have been more women accepted as nurses.

Though these requirements would seem to fit many of the Catholic sisters and nuns serving in the war, Dix also had a "no Catholics need apply" proviso. So the Daughters of Charity operated independently, and doctors found them a pleasant alternative to Dix and her nurses. Plus, the Daughters were the most experienced nurses in the country. They had been nursing and administering hospitals for decades and they had dealt with large-scale public health crises like yellow fever and cholera.

The old Hessian Barracks in Frederick served as the city's largest hospital during the Civil War.

Giving aid in Frederick

The sisters were soon called up for help at other locations, including Manassas, Antietam, and Gettysburg. Despite the feeling that nursing wasn't women's work and a general bias against Catholics, the Daughters of Charity and other Catholic sisters provided valuable service to the soldiers.

Mary Livermore, who worked with a sanitary commission during the war, wrote years later:

> "I am neither a Catholic, nor an advocate of the monastic institutions of that church. Similar organizations established on the basis of the Protestant religion, and in harmony with republican principles, might be made very helpful to modern society, and would furnish occupation and give position to large numbers of unmarried women, whose hearts go out to the work in charitable intent. But I can never forget my experience during the War of Rebellion. Never did I meet these Catholic sisters in hospitals, on transports, on hospital steamers, without observing their devotion, faithfulness, and unobtrusiveness. They gave themselves no airs of superiority or holiness, shirked no duty, sought no easy place, bred no mischiefs. Sick and wounded men watched for their entrance into the wards at morning, and looked a regretful farewell when they departed at night. They broke down in exhaustion from overwork, as did the Protestant nurses; like them, they succumbed to the fatal prison-fever, which our exchanged prisoners brought from the fearful pens of the South."

As the Confederate Army crossed the Potomac River and marched north in September 1862, it soon became clear they were heading towards Frederick. Before the Confederate Army even arrived, citizens of Frederick were seeing refugees flow into the city from the south. Meanwhile, many city residents were heading further north, away from the city.

Patients from the United States Military Hospital, located

in the old Hessian Barracks, where the Daughters of Charity had been working since June 4, were among those evacuated from the city.

Confederate troops marching south on North Market Street in Frederick during the Civil War. Photo courtesy of the Historical Society of Frederick County, Maryland.

As the Confederate Army approached on September 5, the sister in charge of the Daughters of Charity in Frederick hurried into their room and woke them. The hospital was being evacuated. The Confederate Army was in Maryland, and all the patients who could be evacuated were leaving, as well as the male attendants and any male employees at the hospital. The hospital was expected to be evacuated within an hour.

"Imagine our feelings at such news! The hour passed like a flash; the soldiers had all disappeared except a few badly wounded, who could not be removed. The signal was given and in a few moments we beheld the entire city, as it were, enveloped in flames and smoke, so great was the conflagration of the military stores. O, my God! May we never again behold such a sight," Sister Matilda Coskery wrote. The doctors who remained behind to care for those soldiers too sick to be moved brought their instruments and other items of value to the sisters for safekeeping, not only trusting the sisters with their safeguarding but knowing they would not be searched or robbed by the Confederate Army.

The next morning dawned quietly. Few remained on the hospital grounds and those that did awaited the inevitable coming of the invading army. One sick soldier told the sisters, "Oh, Sisters, did you stay to [take] care of us? We thought you would have gone, and then what would have become of us?"

Later that morning, two Confederate cavalrymen galloped into the town shouting, "Jefferson Davis!" and "The time of your delivery has come!" Col. Bradley Johnson and 150 horsemen soon followed. Military bands played "Maryland, My Maryland" and "Dixie" as the Southern troops marched into Frederick. Gen. Stonewall Jackson's advance force of 5,000 men marched up Market Street and camped on the north side of town.

At the hospital, a Confederate officer demanded that the doctors surrender the facility to the Confederate Army, which they did. The Confederate soldiers accepted the surrender and brought about 400 of their own sick and wounded into the hospital.

The Daughters of Charity who were working at the hospital were not only shocked at the condition of the men who were brought in for their care, but also at the condition of those who were bringing them to the hospital. The men told the sisters they had survived on green corn for the previous two weeks. They were "young and old men, with boys who seemed like mere children, emaciated with hunger and covered with tattered rags that gave them more the appearance of dead men than living ones."

The sisters had begun to administer to the ill Confederates when the chief surgeon told them that as employees of the Union government, they couldn't give aid to the Confederates soldiers.

Part of the problem the sisters faced was that the Maryland General Assembly had passed a treason bill in the spring. The new law made it illegal for state and federal workers to provide aid and comfort to the enemy. Since the Daughters of Charity who served in the war were considered federal workers, even if many of them volunteered their services, they could not give aid to the Confederate soldiers or they would find themselves arrested and unable to give aid to anyone, Confederate or Union. For eight days, the sisters could do nothing to ease the Confederates' suffering.

Townspeople weren't so bound and they provided cakes to the soldiers, but in some cases, the rich foods were too much for the starving men and proved fatal. Young men in the nearby Jesuit novitiate volunteered to nurse the sick and "happily their services were accepted by the U.S. Surgeon, who fixed accommodations for them to stay at the barracks," one of the sisters wrote.

On September 11, two sisters got a pass from General Robert E. Lee to travel to Emmitsburg to inform their superiors of the situation in Frederick.

In the meantime, Maj. Gen. George B. McClellan had gathered the Army of the Potomac and headed after the Confederate Army. This led to the army leaving Frederick and heading west over South Mountain. By the time the sisters returned from Emmitsburg, Frederick had been abandoned by the Confederates. At that point, the doctors made no distinction between Union and Confederate soldiers and helped anyone who needed it.

One sister wrote that the soldiers wrote that the soldiers "lay side by side so that we had it in our power to give them equal attention. It was truly edifying to see the patience and harmony that reigned among them. Sometimes they would say, 'Sister, we are not enemies except on the battlefield.'"

A Daughter of Charity cares for a sick soldier in a hospital. Courtesy of the Library of Congress.

Aid post-Antietam

McClellan caught up with Lee's army on South Mountain and the two armies began fighting. The Confederate Army tried to block the Union at the mountain passes without success. McClellan's men pushed through the passes and over the mountain.

The Confederate Army retreated to the west and Lee considered heading south. But with Gen. Stonewall Jackson's capture of Harpers Ferry on September 15, General Lee decided to make a stand at Sharpsburg.

On September 17, a foggy morning, cannons and rifle fire erupted between the towns of Boonsboro and Sharpsburg. So began a twelve-hour battle that would be become the deadliest single day for America. Nearly 100,000 soldiers would eventually fight that day and by day's end, nearly 23,000 would be casualties.

The following day began the work to save the wounded and bury the dead.

Maryland authorities had already requested help from the Daughters of Charity to help with the wounded on the day of the battle. "The people of the area were asked to help the Confederate soldiers, and the Sisters and people of Emmitsburg collected clothing, provisions, remedies, and money."

Father Edward Smith, C.M., pastor in Emmitsburg, drove two sisters to Boonsboro in a wagon. They arrived at twilight after the battle's end and found four hospitals for Union wounded and three for Confederate wounded. "But as the fighting had been over twelve or fifteen miles space, the towns of Boonsboro and Sharpsburg were hospitals," wrote Sister Matilda.

When the Daughters of Charity arrived, two Union officers recognized the sisters by their cornettes and one said, "Ah, there come the Sisters of Charity; now the poor men will be equally cared for."

The sisters headed immediately to the battlefield to search for wounded among the many dead bodies. On their way there, they found all the houses and barns being used as hospitals with the wooden fencing, where there was still any left, draped with bloody clothing. The wounded lay on the ground with only a bit of straw for a mattress. If they were lucky, a blanket might have been stretched out on sticks driven into the ground to provide shade. Otherwise, they had had no protection from the sun during the day as they suffered from their wounds.

The battle's 23,000 casualties nearly overwhelmed the sisters' ability to help them. Someone always seemed to need their attention. No matter how fast they were able to offer help to one soldier, there were always two more waiting.

In Frederick, where the Daughters of Charity were once again able to administer to both Union and Confederate soldiers, the United States Hospital filled quickly with wounded from the battle. The U.S. government ordered churches and other buildings in the city turned into hospitals. The Jesuit Novitiate and Visitation Academy were among them.

"Here was a scene of carnage not to be described; the two armies who had so exultingly passed our windows but a few days before, now returned weltering in each other's gore. What a reflection for the human mind! Could man only comprehend the horrors of Fratricidal War, it would be enough to prevent him from engaging in it ever!" one of the Daughters of Charity wrote.

For the next six weeks, the sisters worked with little rest as they worked to care for the patients.

The result of all the sisters' hard work was that Catholic bias was torn down across the country and the Daughters of Charity became firmly established as healthcare providers.

Spies on the Mountain

T he sailors getting specialized training at Miami University in Ohio gathered in the campus auditorium. They waited uncertainly, not knowing what to expect since their training was not yet done.

Lt. Greene walked onto the stage and asked the group if anyone could speak a foreign language. Hands rose among the sailors in the audience.

Spiro Cappony's hand was among those that went up. He was a young 19-year-old who had become so caught up in patriotic fervor after watching the movie "Wake Island" that he enlisted in the U.S. Navy to fight for his country. As a first-generation American, he could speak the language of his parents, Greek.

Cappony and the sailors who had raised their hands were separated from the main group and interviewed. Once the interviewer found out Cappony spoke Greek, he asked, "Would you like to try something different?" Cappony recalled during a November 2007 phone interview.

"What?" Cappony asked the interviewer.

"Would you like to become a paratrooper?"

Unsure of what he had heard, Cappony said, "I'm in the Navy, sir."

The interviewer nodded. "Well, this is something different. It's a special training course."

"If I have to, I have to," Cappony said, shrugging.

So began Cappony's journey as an agent for the Office of Strategic Services, the forerunner of the Central Intelligence Agency, during WWII.

The OSS

"The Office of Strategic Services was the first effort by this country at unorthodox warfare and strategic intelligence. Prior to that time, the army and navy had what we called tactical intelligence that had to do with battlefield intelligence and the like, but [William] Donovan felt and convinced the president that we had to know what the capabilities and the intentions of other nations were from a strategic point of view," William Putzell, Jr. said in his interview for the Library of Congress' Veterans History Project.

The seal of the Office of Strategic Services. Courtesy of the CIA.

Donovan was a highly decorated veteran who had gone into a private law practice until President Franklin D. Roosevelt called him back to serve his country and put together the new intelligence-gathering unit.

"He's [Donovan's] the only one in my limited experience that had physical and intellectual daring in one person. You usually see one or the other but not both," Putzell said.

At its peak in late 1944, the OSS employed nearly 13,000 civilians and military personnel, according to the CIA website. About 7,500 of them served overseas, and approximately

4,500 of the employees were women (and 900 of them served overseas). Over its four-year life, the OSS spent about $135 million, or nearly $3 billion in current dollars, to gather enemy intelligence and disrupt their operations.

Recruits arrive at the OSS training camp on Catoctin Mountain. Screenshot from an OSS film.

Catoctin Recreational Demonstration Area

The OSS maintained training camps in Virginia, Maryland, and Canada. The Maryland site was located on Catoctin Mountain in Frederick County. The location was about an hour north of Washington, D.C. and next door to President Roosevelt's retreat that he called Shangri-La.

The Catoctin Recreational Demonstration Area had been a popular summer camp for groups like the League for Crippled Children and The Salvation Army. On April 5, 1942, the swing arm gates of the park swung shut and were locked. A notice ran in the newspapers notifying readers, "The Catoctin Area is Ordered Closed to the Public." Armed guards stood watch to make sure they stayed that way. Once the gates were closed, former Catoctin Mountain Park Ranger Debra Mills said those groups were "given notice that the summer camping season was canceled and no future use could be guaranteed."

The residents of Frederick County had become used to a military presence on Catoctin Mountain. In the summer of 1941, a temporary training camp had been set up in the Catoctin Recreational Demonstration Area and soldiers set up their tents next to the CCC barracks already on the mountain. British sailors also enjoyed a break from the war and used the park for recreation, according to national park records.

Although Catoctin Mountain Park was leased to the War Department, "The park superintendents remained on duty to continue the National Park Service's primary mission: to preserve the natural resources for future generations of Americans. Under the terms of the lease, the War Department agreed to uphold the Park's prohibitions on the destruction of trees, shrubs, and wildlife, and to restore the Park's facilities at the end of the war," John Whiteclay Chambers, II, wrote in Catoctin History.

Because of the government's need for training camps, it had turned to the National Park Service and, in particular, recreation demonstration areas for land to create temporary camps. RDAs were generally located near urban areas and had camp facilities in them, but they were still primitive enough that having thousands of men tramp over them wouldn't cause permanent damage.

Then trains began arriving and stopping at Lantz, Md., to unload men and women who entered the guarded camp. Others began arriving by truck.

"We got into a truck in Washington (D.C.) that had the side flaps down. We didn't know where we were going," Frank Gleason said during an October 2007 phone interview. Gleason had been a demolitions instructor at Area B.

Most of the recruits arriving at Area B had already completed preliminary training at another OSS camp in what is currently Prince William Forest Park in Virginia.

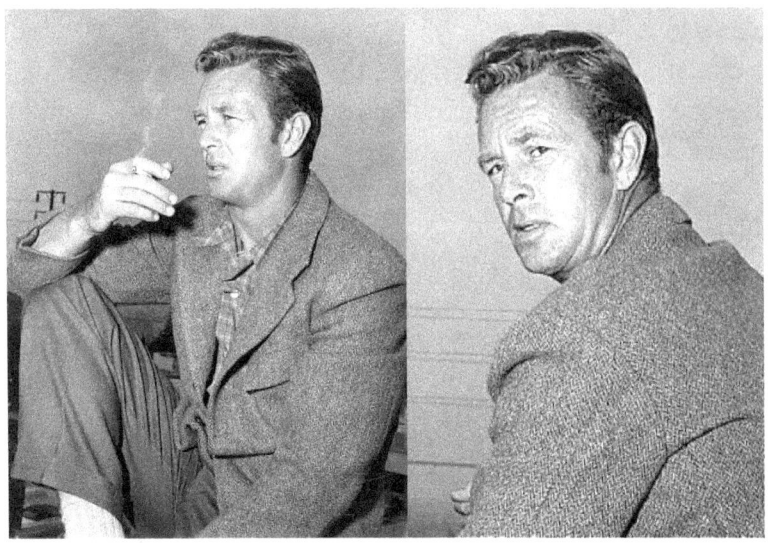

Actor Sterling Hayden was an OSS agent who trained at Catoctin Mountain Park. Photo courtesy of Wikimedia Commons.

The Recruits

Military recruits like Cappony and Gleason were the people the OSS usually recruited, but that was not always the case. Chambers said many young men were recruited from top universities and society families to be trained as spies. However, to learn needed skills, they mixed with criminals who taught things like safecracking and forgery.

Women were also among the recruits. "The women, most of them that became—went into the Secret Service were American citizens, but they had backgrounds of French or English or German. And so it was very easy to give them a passport, again, of that nationality. So technically, no, no American woman went into combat or went into the intelligence, parachuted in. But in actuality, they did," former OSS agent Rafael Hirtz said in his interview for the National History Project.

Area B

Maj. Ainsworth Blogg was the first commander of Area B. The OSS had recruited him from the Army Reserves around the same time that the park was closed to the public.

Recruits working out on the trainazium. Screenshot from the OSS film about Area B.

Camp Greentop was used as a training school, and the administrative center was located in Camp Round Meadow. Both of these used existing facilities. Some specialized facilities, such as firing ranges and obstacle courses, needed to be constructed to turn the national park into a place that could train recruits in a basic paramilitary course.

One unique obstacle course was called a "trainazium." Six telephone-pole-size logs were set into the ground and connected by smaller poles 18 feet above the ground. An old film of the trainazium shows recruits swinging, running, and climbing at the top of the trainazium.

Gleason was quoted in Catoctin History as saying, the trainazium was used "to build the men's self-confidence, to build up their physical strength and dexterity...and [teach them] to be agile on narrow high places."

Another unique training feature camp was called the "House of Horrors." It was a windowless building "filled with wobbly walkways, moving objects, sound effects, flashing lights, and other surprises," Chambers wrote. Trainees, armed with a .45-caliber pistol and two clips of six rounds, were sent into the house at night. As the trainees crept through the house, cardboard cutouts of Nazis popped into the open, requiring trainees to think fast and shoot them, according to the Catoctin Mountain Park website.

Edgar Prichard, a recruit at Area B, said in Catoctin History, "Each of us over a period of a couple of days would be awakened in the middle of the night and hauled off to carry out a special mission. When it came my time, I was told that there was a Nazi soldier holed up in a building and that it was my job to go in and kill him. I was given a .45 and two clips [of ammunition]. The house I was sent into was a log house with long corridors and stairways. I wasn't sure whether there really was a Nazi soldier there or not. I kicked a door open with my gun at the ready. Paper targets with photographs of uniformed German soldiers jumped out at me from every corner and every window and doorway. We had been taught to always fire two shots at the target. There must have been six targets because I got two bullets in each one. The last one was a dummy sitting in a chair with a lighted cigarette in his hand. If you didn't shoot him, you failed the test."

Area B instructors like Gleason trained OSS agents in hand-to-hand combat, infiltration training, marksmanship and setting charges. Other instruction included creating disguises, concealing microfilm, and recruiting resistance agents. "Students tested different explosives and fuses on pieces of iron, steel, and wood as practice for blowing up bridges, dams, railroad radio towers or power plants," Chambers wrote.

"We trained in individual sabotage," Gleason said. "It's what the terrorists do now. It was fascinating work. Our job was to interfere with the enemy in every way possible."

The House of Horrors at Area B. Screenshot from the OSS film about Area B.

At any given time, the camp would have about 100 recruits who were spending two weeks in training on the mountain, according to the Catoctin Mountain Park website. However, the site could accommodate up to 250 trainees, plus staff, according to Chambers, who based his estimate on layout maps of the buildings in the camp.

Cappony said that one of the first assignments he was given when he arrived at Area B was to "bust up rocks like we were convicts. It was a test of our endurance and our minds to see if they could get to us."

Cappony's training allowed him to pack on muscle until he weighed 180 pounds.

"I became a tough, little guy," he said. "I learned about knife throwing, how to kill with my bare hands, how to kill with a newspaper or a comb."

Cappony trained with the man who had recruited him into the OSS, Capt. John Hamilton. By the time they arrived at Area B, Cappony already knew that John Hamilton was actually movie actor Sterling Hayden. He would also go on to fight the Germans in Yugoslavia.

"We didn't know anyone by their real names," said Albert Guay in a November 2007 phone interview. He worked as a company clerk at Area B for a few months.

During training, none of the recruits used their real names—even to those in their group. Instead, aliases allowed for a cloak of secrecy. Among the expert training staff was a colorful English colonel, formerly employed by the Shanghai police. The colonel was remembered as a particularly "notorious character in the OSS," according to the Catoctin Mountain Park website.

Recruits were sometimes injured during training. In one incident, trainees were told to crawl along a path as small explosions detonated overhead, simulating combat. According to Chambers, William Casey, a young lawyer from New York, rose up too soon.

"An explosion knocked a piece of wood from the tree about the size of a football," Chambers said. "It hit him in the face and broke his jaw."

That young trainee grew up to become director of the CIA under President Reagan.

"Many people who later became directors of the CIA had commando training here in Catoctin," Chambers said.

During the 4- to 6-week training course, the trainees' days lasted from 6 a.m. to 11 p.m. with actual training running from 7 a.m. to 5 p.m. six days a week.

"When we were well trained, I could take a group of six people and put a major city out of action for a month," Gleason said. "You blow up the sewers, blow up power plants, and destroy the motors for phones."

American agents weren't the only ones who trained at Area B. Recruits came from Norway, Thailand, Yugoslavia, Italy, and France and went through the rigorous training at Catoctin, according to Chambers.

After completing OSS training, the agents' "final project" was to infiltrate various military targets in the region, such as shipyards and steel mills. According to Chambers, William Peers and Nicol Smith were able to get into the Fairchild Aircraft factory in Hagerstown in 1942 and return not only with the layout of the factory, but with a plan for how to sabotage it.

If the trainees were successful, like Peers and Smith, they were sent into the field.

Taking a break

The trainees weren't always stuck in camp during their training. They traveled to nearby towns for a drink or USO dances where they could enjoy the company of pretty girls.

"They would load us on the truck and take us into Thurmont, Hagerstown, and Frederick on weekends and evenings," Guay said.

When asked where they were from, the soldiers always said Fort Ritchie, which was an army fort north of the OSS camp.

"It was supposed to be a secret, but it didn't take long to know that everyone already knew," Guay said. "It wasn't much of a secret."

Behind enemy lines

Once the agents were trained, many of them had their training put to the test when they were sent behind enemy lines.

In 1943, Cappony shipped out to Cairo, Egypt. He did parachute training in Palestine before being sent to work in the embassy in Istanbul, Turkey. While at the embassy, Cappony found out that Turkey was funneling ore to Germany via supply lines. Cappony set out to disrupt those operations. He spent nine months in northern Greece working with Greek guerrillas. They blew up bridges, engaged in counterattacks and did everything they could to harass the Germans.

"I knew I had been trained to protect myself. I was in dangerous territory. I knew I could be mean, quick, and protect myself. I knew I had to be good, or I'd be dead," Cappony said.

Not all the agents were successful. Some paid the ultimate price. "In March 1944, all fifteen members of a sabotage team of Italian Americans from the OSS Italian Operational Group that had trained at Area B were caught and executed by the Nazis in an open field in northern Italy," Chambers wrote.

Chambers said his research has led him to believe, "The OSS had a significant role in helping the Allies to win the war."

As for the history of the OSS, information is beginning to dribble out as more and more documents are declassified. With more information available, the men and women of the OSS are being recognized for their service.

Guay, who got out of the OSS after a few months, said, "Looking back, I think I made a big mistake. I had no idea what that would turn into."

In 2007, the Greek Embassy honored Cappony and the other agents who served behind enemy lines.

Gen. Hap Holliday awards Spiro Cappony the Bronze Star for his actions as an OSS agent. Photo courtesy of the Veterans History Project.

End of the war

The OSS closed Area B in June 1944, and Camp Ritchie took over the training areas to use for its Army Military Intelligence Training School.

Once the war ended, the process of returning the park to civilian use began. Camp Ritchie Army Engineers removed the munitions and firing range and dismantled the House of Horrors and trainazium. They also had to examine the training areas to remove booby traps and unexploded grenades and mortar shells.

Because the heavy traffic on Catoctin Mountain had damaged the main road to the park that was located near Lantz, a new road was constructed. This road was designated Route 77, and a new entrance to the park was built off of it.

Area B today

Very little remains to show the military's presence in Catoctin Mountain Park. The OSS winterized the camping cabins, and the mountain is now home to a state park, a national park, and Camp David.

"We have found one mortar round that could have been from the training done up here," said former Catoctin Mountain Park Superintendent Mel Poole.

Poole said that it's been known the park was an OSS camp for years, but it has only been in recent years that it has become known what the OSS was.

"I think the real trigger to realizing what went on here was when I went to the International Spy Museum," Poole said. "I was standing next to James Bond's Aston Martin, and they were showing a continuous loop of a film shot here on Catoctin Mountain by [Academy Award-Winning Director] John Ford about what they did here."

The film shows the training of the agents at Area B and even places like the House of Horrors. However, all the recruits in the movie wear "Lone Ranger" masks so that they can't be identified.

The National Park Service is still trying to piece together the details of life in the camp.

"We always thought people came in by the road they use now," Poole said. "When we took a former agent around, he didn't recognize the place until we went up by Lantz. Then he said, 'This is the way we came and went in the park.'"

Once the former agent was oriented, he was able to identify many of the areas of Area B and explain to the park staff what they had been used for.

Still, not everything is known about Area B's history. Catoctin Mountain Park holds onto some of its secrets just as tightly as the OSS did.

ODDS & ENDS

Frederick County was the first to say "no" to unfair taxation

Most people wouldn't think of Frederick County as a place where the American Revolution was fomented. It is often forgotten amid other places like Boston and Philadelphia.

However, when the British Parliament passed the Stamp Act in 1765, the American colonists were not happy when the news reached them. The Stamp Act revenue was supposed to finance the costs of keeping British troops in North America. It was the first internal tax levied directly on American colonies. It required all official documents in the colonies be printed on a specially stamped paper.

The news of this tax reached Maryland in May 1765, when the text of the act was printed in The (Annapolis) Maryland Gazette. Newspapers like the Gazette opposed the act because they also would have to be printed on the taxed paper, increasing their costs.

The stamped paper arrived in Maryland in October 1764, shortly before the act was to take effect November 1. Mike Maharrey wrote in a Tenth Amendment Center article that between May and October the citizens' anger over the Stamp Act had "reached the point that Gov. Horatio Sharpe was afraid the colonists would destroy the paper if it was offloaded. He requested that the stamped paper remain onboard the ship until the situation cooled off. As a result, when November 1, the effective date of the Stamp Act, rolled around, there was no stamped paper available in the

Maryland colony."

In mid-November 1764, 12 magistrates of the Frederick County court ordered a man to be released on bail and directed court clerk John Darnall to draw up the paperwork for the court. With no official stamped paper available, Darnall said that his office couldn't conduct any official business until it received the paper, essentially bringing legal and commercial business to a halt in the county.

A cartoon against the Stamp Act published in the Pennsylvania Journal in 1765. Courtesy of the Library of Congress.

The magistrates ordered him to continue without the stamped paper. When Darnall refused, he was found in contempt of court and jailed. After a night in jail, he said he would comply, paid a fine, and was released.

On November 23, the magistrates unanimously ruled that the Stamp Act would be ignored. The stated two reasons for this decision were: 1) There had been no formal notice of the act's passage and implementation, and 2) It was impractical to halt all business in the county because no stamped paper was available.

Their ruling read, in part: "It is the unanimous resolution and opinion of this Court that all business thereof shall and ought to be transacted in the usual and accustom manner without any inconvenience or delay to be occasioned from the want of stamped paper, parchment of vellum and that all proceedings shall be valid and effectual without the use of stamps, and they enjoin and order all sheriffs, clerks, counsellors, attorneys and all officers of the court to proceed in their several avocations as usual which resolution and opinion are grounded on the following reasons."

This was the first act of revolt against the Stamp Act, and it was done by simply ignoring it.

Some historians believe this act of repudiation was actually a bit of theatrics.

"Darnall had served in that capacity as court clerk since the founding of the county in 1748. One of the sitting magistrates for the November 1765 Court Term was James Dickson, who was Darnall's son-in-law. As Millard M. Rice points out in his book This Was the Life, a careful reading of the court proceedings prior to Nov. 18, 1765 shows no evidence of anyone at the Frederick County Court having a concern about conducting legal business without the Stamp Act paper. The justices selected one seemingly insignificant case on which to make their ruling. The justices refer to 'this Province,' implying an expansion beyond the boundaries of Frederick County, and an indication there may have been others, at a higher level of government, involved in formulating the decision. One can speculate the justices, besides seeking an opportunity to snub the Stamp Act, also were providing Darnall some political cover by 'forcing' him to accept the court's ruling," Ryan Bass and Pat Barron wrote in their article "Repudiation of the Stamp Act."

The 12 magistrates who defied the law have become known as "The Twelve Immortals." They are: Thomas Beatty, Peter Bainbridge, Josiah Beall, Samuel Beall, William Blair, James Dickson, Andrew Heugh, Charles Jones, William Luckett, David Lynn, Thomas Price and Joseph Smith.

A week after they took their stand against unfair taxation, the people of Frederick Town showed their support. They held a mock funeral where they buried a copy of the Stamp Act with an effigy of a royal tax collector on the grounds of the county courthouse, which is now where the Frederick City Hall is located. The "Colours of the Towns Company" and drummers led the procession, followed by the townspeople, who carried a large banner followed by a coffin covered in anti-Stamp Act slogans. This was followed by an effigy of the tax collector, who was the sole mourner and the Sons of Liberty "two and two."

"The STAMP-ACT having received a mortal wound by the Hands of Justice, on Saturday last gave up the Ghost, to the great joy of the Inhabitants of Frederick County. The lifeless body lay exposed to public Ignominy 'til Yesterday, when it was thought proper, for preventing infection-from its stench to bury it in the following manner…," according to The (Annapolis) Maryland Gazette.

This defiance inspired other places to do similar things by capturing or destroying the stamped paper and forcing officials to have to make decisions to ignore the Stamp Act. This led to colonial assemblies passing resolutions that spoke of the natural rights of colonists and stated that the Stamp Act was unlawful and void.

The British Parliament repealed the act on March 18, 1766, without it ever having been effectively enforced.

In 1894, the Maryland General Assembly made November 23, a bank half-holiday in Frederick County to celebrate Repudiation Day, the day when the Twelve Immortals repudiated the Stamp Act.

In 1904, the Frederick Chapter of the Daughters of the American Revolution placed a plaque listing the names of the twelve magistrates in the Frederick County Courthouse.

The Last Trolley to Thurmont

t only 46 years old, the Thurmont trolley was the last of its kind. The popularity of automobiles and buses and the improvements in roads had evolved transportation, leaving inter-urban trolleys, like the Thurmont trolley, a dinosaur nearing extinction.

"The last interurban passenger trolley in Maryland, the Frederick-Thurmont line, will roll into discard and the occasion can only put mist in the eye and a sentimental ache in the heart of the middle aged," Betty Sullivan wrote in The Frederick Post on February 20, 1954. "To them the clang, clang, clang of the trolley turns thoughts backward in a time when life still centered in the local community and a twenty-mile journey was a venture abroad to be undertaken with forethought and definite plan."

The trolley had transported 3.8 million riders around Frederick County in 1920, but by 1940, that number was down to 500,000 riders.

"Gradually the bus and the passenger car snipped away at trolley patronage, gradually lines were discontinued, until the 17-mile stretch from Frederick to Thurmont was the only link in the state between two such urban points," Sullivan wrote. "Despite competition this trolley kept its faithful friends and some 60 commuters will use it until the final day."

The final day was February 20, 1954.

"After February 20, the Frederick-Thurmont route will be converted into a bus line for passengers and a regular railroad freight car will be substituted onto the tracks to handle freight," reported The (Hagerstown) Daily Mail.

Once the ending of service was announced, business on the trolley picked up so much that a Sunday service was added for the first time in years.

"One of the trolleys was chartered last Sunday by the Washington Railway Historical Society. On Saturday, so many passengers showed up that a double header was required for one round trip," reported The (Hagerstown) Daily Mail.

H&F RR No. 171 waits as the crowd listens to the remarks being made by Potomac Edison officials and local representatives before its final trip. Photo courtesy of Thurmontimages.com.

The Thurmont trolley began life in 1886 when the Monocacy Valley Railroad Company built a steam train line to haul iron from Catoctin Furnace to Thurmont and the Western Maryland Railroad. Two years later, the Northern Railroad Company extended the line to Frederick. In 1908, the lines became electric. Finally, in 1913, the Northern Railway Company connected to the Washington County railroad lines and the Hagerstown and Frederick Railway Company was formed.

The Thurmont trolley was unique because it operated on tracks that were of regular width for trains. Trolleys generally used narrower rails.

The two final trolleys left the car barn in Frederick with about 100 invited guests on a Saturday morning that was drizzling rain. Each passenger had a souvenir ticket punched in regulation fashion. Flags and bunting were hung along the route and photographers followed the progress of the trolley, snapping pictures.

"Uncounted hundreds of rolls of film were consumed during the event, by dozens of people who turned out at every hamlet along the trolley's route, and by the passengers. Some persons brought along movie cameras. One unidentified man drove from Allentown, Pa., in time to accompany the trolley to Thurmont and back, via auto. Driving along the roads that came closest to the trolley's tracks, he made an endless series of moving picture scents of the vehicle in progress, because his hobby consists of taking pictures of trolley cars," reported The (Hagerstown) Daily Mail.

Though the outside of the cars were decorated, very little had changed inside them. One report noted that the leather hand straps riders could hold on to were as good as new. This was because the cars were rarely crowded enough for them to be used. "But the rest of the trolley equipment has an antiquated atmosphere. The no-spitting sign is yellow with ade. Some of the advertising signs had been there since the days of World War Two, because they referred to beer that would still lead the field after peace came," reported The (Hagerstown) Daily Mail.

During the ride, the former riders recounted their stories of the trolley.

The ride to Thurmont took a little more than an hour where the passengers were greeted by a crowd of about 100 people. Thurmont Mayor Ray Weddle, Jr.; Potomac Edison President R. Paul Smith and Frederick Mayor Donald Rice made short remarks to the gathering because of the rain.

The crowd gathers to listen to speaker including R. Paul Smith, President of Potomac Edison, the parent company of the H&F RR at the microphone and Thurmont Mayor Ray Weddle at the right. Photo courtesy of Thurmontimages.com.

On the return trip, The (Hagerstown) Daily Mail noted, "Passengers sang 'I've Been Working on the Railroad' and 'Auld Lang Syne' and stops were made at two points— Yellow Springs and Lewistown."

"Officially it ended at 1:30 Saturday afternoon when a

hundred invited guests climbed down from Potomac Edison Co. veteran cars No. 171 and No. 172 in the East Patrick Street car barn after completing the 34-mile round trip to Thurmont that had many of the aspects of a big parade," reported The Frederick Post.

When the trolleys returned, buses took the passengers to a luncheon at the Francis Scott Key Hotel. During the luncheon Smith said, "Progress eventually overtakes all of man's previous works. This is true in existence of the trolley car, as it was when it first came into being. The passing of the trolley closes, except in our memories and to those contributions to our lives both socially and economically, a great era of expansion and development."

Though the trolley service ended, its impact on the region is still felt. Because of the power demands for electric trolleys, their existence necessitated the creation of a high-capacity power generating plant. It's this power network that grew profitable while the trolleys it powered became less profitable. The Hagerstown and Frederick Railway became the Potomac Edison Company in 1923.

"Oddly, that was the trolley's salvation. By the early 1930s, the rail network was economically obsolete and parts were abandoned by Potomac Edison, including half of the Frederick-Hagerstown 'main line.' But the big and wealthy utility seemingly could not face discarding its onetime parent entirely, and three routes survived into the late 1940s," Herbert Harwood Jr. wrote in an article for the Maryland Department of Energy about the Hagerstown and Frederick Railway.

The trolley also had a small role in the building of Interstate 70. The (Hagerstown) Morning Herald reported on February 27, 1954, the one of the Thurmont trolleys would be loaned to the Maryland State Roads Commission. "The State Roads Commission will use it for office purposes at Frederick. Work is being rushed on the completion of a new dual highway between Frederick and Baltimore, and the officials who are overseeing its completion will set up their desks and records inside the sturdily constructed trolley car," the newspaper reported.

Freight service continued on the line until 1958, when the tracks were finally removed.

Potomac Edison President R. Paul Smith boards the trolley at the car barn in Frederick for the last trip to Thurmont. Photo courtesy of Thurmontimages.com.

The Greatest Killer in the World

A lthough the country essentially quarantined itself in 2020, it's not the first time such a thing has happened. However, when it happened in 1918, 675,000 Americans died in roughly two months. Worldwide, the death toll may have reached 100 million people or one person out of every 20.

Spanish Flu is the worst disease the world has ever known.

Much like COVID-19, when Spanish Flu was noticed and when it began are two different times. It first appeared in Spain in February 1918, hence, the name. However, because Spain was a neutral country during World War I, the press was free to report on the flu, although other places were said to be having troubles with the disease. One historian believes he traced the flu back to a Chinese avian flu in 1917.

With this first wave of the Spanish Flu, people got fever, chills, and aches for three days, and then they would be fine. It was 1918's seasonal flu, and there was nothing to be concerned about except that more people than usual caught the disease. The odd thing about the flu of 1918 is that rather than attacking the very old and very young with weaker immune systems, it also attacked healthy adults in their 30s and 40s.

The flu spread worldwide, including the United States when it appeared at Camp Funston in Kansas in March. Because flu was not a reportable disease, it's uncertain how many cases there were, but 233 soldiers developed pneumonia, and 48 doughboys died. Given the number of soldiers in camp, this was not considered a remarkable mortality rate.

With a virulent flu sidelining so many soldiers across the world, it affected the progress of WWI. However, the flu vanished as temperatures warmed.

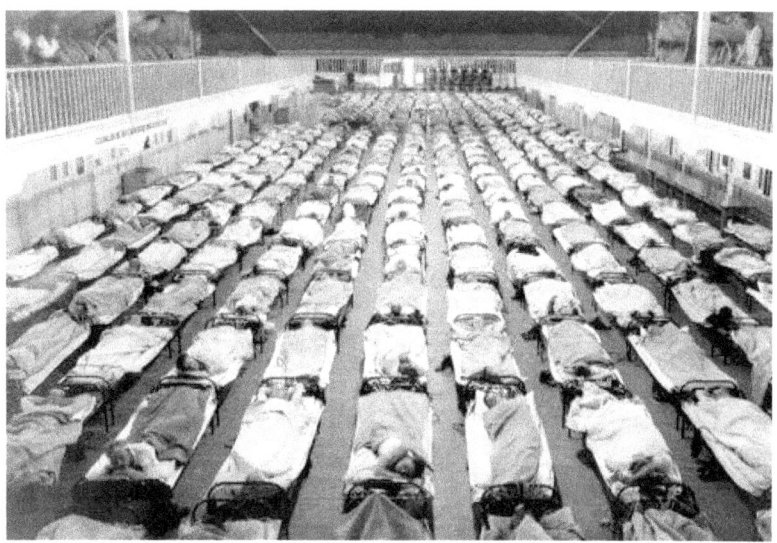

An emergency hospital set up for patients with Spanish Flu in Kansas. Photo courtesy of the Library of Congress.

The deadly flu

Spanish Flu appeared again in late August. This time, it was even more contagious and much more deadly.

One physician wrote that patients rapidly "develop the most vicious type of pneumonia that has ever been seen," and later when cyanosis appeared in patients "it is simply a struggle for air until they suffocate." Another doctor said the influenza patients "died struggling to clear their airways of a blood-tinged froth that sometimes gushed from their mouth and nose."

The second wave first appeared in America at Boston. On August 28, 1918, eight sailors reported sick with the flu. The next day, the number was 58, and by day four, it was 81. After another week, the number was 119, and civilians were getting sick. On September 8, three people died.

A police officer directing traffic while wearing a mask during the Spanish Flu pandemic. Photo courtesy of the Library of Congress.

By this time, it had spread beyond Boston. Flu reports were coming in along the East Coast.

On September 26, 50,000 residents of Massachusetts had the flu, in Boston alone, 133 died that day from flu and 33 from pneumonia.

In Frederick County

Spanish Flu first appeared in Frederick County around the end of September 1918. On September 20, local newspapers warned that an outbreak was coming. At that time, only one known case of the flu was in Maryland. By September 25, hundreds of cases had been reported, mostly soldiers at Camp Meade, although there was no reference to any in Frederick County.

Given the headlines, Spanish Flu struck suddenly, although no unexpected, in Frederick County. "Spanish Flu Sweeps Co.; Fifty Cases," read The (Frederick) News headline on September 26. The article notes one thing thwarted researchers trying to get an accurate count, and that is that all flu cases weren't being reported to the health officer, either because the doctors were too busy working or because influenza wasn't a disease that they were required to report. By the way, that changed after the Spanish flu outbreak, at least in Maryland.

The following day, 10 more cases were reported. Another early case from Buckeystown involved Sallie Barber traveled from Baltimore to Buckeystown to help care for her parents who had the flu. John Henry Barber became the first known death in the county from the flu on September 28. The next day, Sallie herself was confined to bed from the flu. On September 30, she died. A few days later, her six-year-old daughter died even as other relatives took sick from the flu.

By October 2, more than 100 cases were reported in Buckeystown alone.

At this early stage, Thurmont, Emmitsburg, Urbana, New

Market, and Buckeystown were the hardest hit areas, according to Dr. T. Clyde Routson, the county health officer. He was against closing schools at first because the children would play and mingle with friends and the result would be the same. He also said that it would be unfair to communities not affected to have their children deprived of education.

The Frederick Post headline on October 7 was "Physicians Believe That Epidemic Has Been Checked." This was far from the truth. The flu had taken hold in all areas of the county. During the month of October, a flu story could be found on the front page of The Frederick Post every day it was published, except for two days. Most of those headlines announced how many had died the previous day.

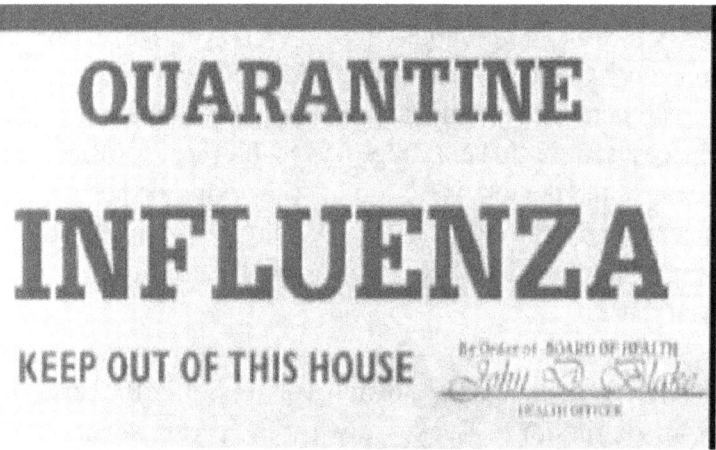

Houses where someone with Spanish Flu lived were often quarantined. Photo courtesy of the Library of Congress.

Quarantining

Frederick County started talking about closing the county's borders on October 7. However, beat them to the punch, theaters, movies, schools, dance halls, another other public places in the state on October 8. Camp Meade, which had been flu free a few weeks earlier had 277 deaths, more than 5 percent of its population. Three Daughters of Charity from Emmitsburg and three from Baltimore had been there since October 3 trying to fight the disease. The sisters reported back two days after arriving that there had been 100 deaths in one day and 30 deaths on their first night at Camp Meade.

Since the Crimean War the previous century, whenever there was a public health crisis, whether in peace or war, the Daughters had been called on to help. Around this time, the Daughters of Charity received telegraph and phone messages from sisters across the country asking for their help.

Also, the first Daughter of Charity died from the flu around this time after being sick only four days. St. Joseph's College in Emmitsburg reported that nearly all the teachers were sick and 31 of the students had the flu.

Suddenly the flu began appearing repeatedly on the front page of the newspapers, although not the lead story generally. WWI was winding down, and so the last battles and then the truce talks were the big stories of the day supposedly.

A deadly October

On October 11, The Frederick Post reported that 50 people in the county had died from the flu, although this seems too low just looking at the daily numbers it was reporting. The newspaper noted on October 12, "There are homes in this city where entire families are ill and bed-ridden with influenza and nobody to help care for them."

County Health Officer T. C. Routson and the Red Cross called on student nurses to help care for the sick. They only had mixed success because many of the young women were afraid to help because they didn't want to catch the flu themselves.

On October 14, The Frederick Post tried a good news, bad news thing. New cases of the flu had "slumped". Yea! However, more people who already had the flu were dying.

Face masks were required to ride public transportation during the Spanish Flu pandemic. Photo courtesy of the Library
of Congress.

By the middle of October, the Daughters of Charity had
sent everyone they could spare from the Central House in

Emmitsburg out to serve in the missions. However, sisters at the Central House were also suffering from the flu.

By October 17, Mount St. Mary's College alone had 160 students and faculty sick with the flu, after first appearing on campus the previous week. Two Daughters of Charity were on the campus trying to help, but it wasn't enough. The situation at the college was so serious that Monsignor Bradley, president of the college, asked Maj. Dwight D. Eisenhower at Camp Colt in Gettysburg for medical assistance. The camp was experiencing its own problems with the flu, but Eisenhower did send two doctors to help. The doctors placed the college under military quarantine, and no one was allowed off the grounds.

Mount St. Mary's College newspaper, The Mountaineer, noted that, "In consequence of this quarantine all students who were free from any sign of the disease were sent to their homes early in December and did not return until January was well advanced."

With only eight deaths on the 17th, The Frederick Post declared that the flu was "waning". It noted in the article that the death rate was lower, but you don't see the higher death rates in the paper except for the one instance. The paper reported on October 18, "With only four deaths yesterday, the average death rate per day, which is usually about nine or ten, has been cut down less than half."

The first student at St. Joseph's College died from the flu on October 18. It was the first pupil death since 1872. The following day, another student died. The following day, a sister serving at Soldier's Home in Washington died and another sister in Emmitsburg died the following day. It looks like four sisters eventually died from the flu, although there may have been more. Certainly more were given the Last Rites.

A week later, the newspaper reported that there had only been two flu deaths in the county the previous day. "This is the smallest number of victims for a single day since the influenza became an epidemic." Sadly, the doctor in charge of the main Red Cross hospital had fallen victim of the flu and died.

The county fairs in both Frederick and Washington counties wound up being canceled that year reluctantly. The directors argued that the fresh air would do people good. However, in the end, they must have realized that attendance would be down because people were sick, and many healthy people would be afraid to be part of a crowd for fear of catching the flu.

It was only the second time that the Great Frederick Fair had been canceled. The only time previously that the fair had been canceled was when a little spat called the Civil War happened.

Churches decided to prevent parishioners from being close to each other.

Also, volunteer nurses were being sent throughout the county to visit the homes where entire families were down with the flu. They would care for these families in their homes.

The B&O Railroad brought in its emergency hospital to help people in Brunswick, which apparently was one of the harder hit areas of the county. An emergency hospital run by the Red Cross was also set up at minutes.

The perfect storm

Many communities were already shorthanded medically because doctors had been drafted to serve in WWI. Then along came the flu, which intensified by the shortage by making many of the remaining doctors sick at a time when the workload was drastically increasing. The remaining doctors found themselves working longer hours with contagious people. This would wear them down and make them susceptible to flu and the process would repeat.

One example of this can be seen with Dr. Brown and Dr. Kuhlman in Jefferson. They had 30 patients sick with the flu, but they were sick themselves and bedridden. Dr. Brown tried to help his patients over the phone without much luck.

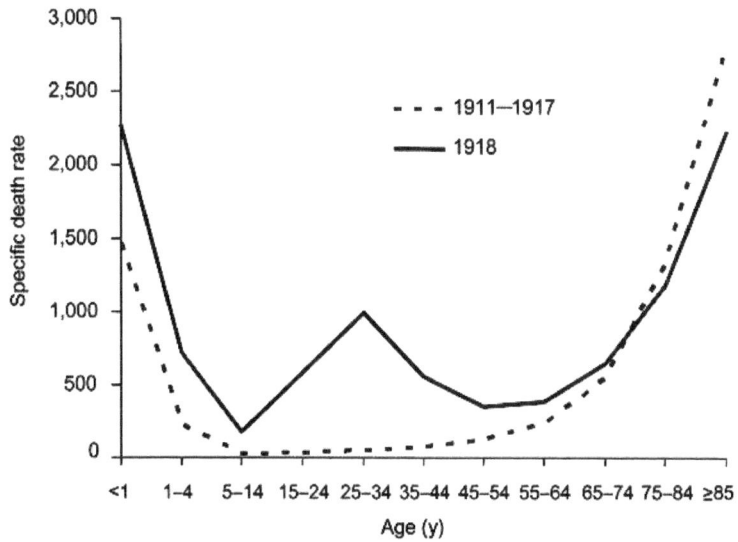

Like most diseases, Spanish Flu disproportionately affected the old and the young, but Spanish Flu also killed those in the prime of their lives.

County Health Officer T. C. Routson noted that Thurmont's efforts to fight the flu were hampered because all the doctors there were sick with the flu. At its peak, Thurmont doctors were seeing 50 to 60 patients a day.

Other professions faced similar problems. An ad in The Frederick Post urged residents not to make unnecessary phone calls. "The influenza epidemic had brought a heavy overload of calls to our wires. It has caused a serious shortage in our operating force. Calls other than those concerning important government work, and those compelled by the epidemic, embarrass the country's war program and place lives in jeopardy."

Even newspaper delivery was affected because many of the carriers were sickened by the flu. In Brunswick, rail service was crippled because "about half of the population has the flu," according to The Frederick Post.

Police officers in Seattle all wore face masks during the Spanish Flu pandemic. Photo courtesy of the Library of Congress.

The third wave

Halloween passed on October 31 without any celebration.

Maryland listed its closure order on November 4. Parts of Frederick County also saw a resurgence of the flu in December, but without any deaths. The Catoctin Clarion in late December reported, "Influenza, a disease dreaded by a big majority of people, is not disappearing very rapidly at this time, the number of cases increasing rather than decreasing in various communities."

Christmas 1918 was somber. A lot of people had lost someone they knew to the flu. Officials urged people to do their shopping early when fewer people would be in the stores. Church Christmas programs were canceled for fear of having too many people in a confined space.

Determining impact

Maryland conducted a door-to-door survey in March 1919 in Baltimore, Cumberland, Lonaconing, Frederick, Salisbury and three rural districts in Frederick, Washington, and Wicomico counties. The information is useful, but not conclusive, which is something that the survey itself noted when it acknowledged some of the shortfalls.

Although deaths didn't exceed births in 1918, it came close with 32,183 deaths, which was about 10,000 more than 5 years in either direction. The death rate was 2257 per 100,000 or about 700 more than the years on either side. No other year from 1902 to present day comes close.

The U.S. Census also reported that the decade between 1910 and 1920 is only decade since 1900 that Frederick County lost population, to which Spanish Flu certainly contributed.

Looking at the Maryland survey, newspaper reports, surrounding county information, and county reports, it appears about 350 people or .7 percent of the county's population died from the flu. However, this might be underestimated because it is known that during the pandemic's peak, some doctors were so overwhelmed they couldn't fill out death certificates until days later, and they sometimes left the cause of death blank.

What is known is that Spanish Flu was the worst disease to hit Frederick County.

Solemn Remembrance

For those in the Walkersville area, a thundering boom that could have been mistaken for a lightning strike interrupted the gray, drizzly morning of May 6, 1981.

Pat Hamilton knew it wasn't lightning, although she wasn't exactly sure what the blast meant. She was helping her husband load a truck when she heard an explosion. "When I heard the noise I looked up, it had burst into flames, and it was still up in the air. It looked like it was just about four houses down from us. I think it was extinguishing itself as it came down because then all I could see was a huge black cloud," Hamilton told The (Frederick) News at the time.

Paul Green Jr. and his wife also heard the explosion. When they looked outside, they saw black smoke rising from a field they farmed. They thought it might have been a train wreck, since the Maryland Midland Railroad ran along the edge of the field, so they climbed into their truck to investigate.

"At first, we thought it was a train, but then we saw pieces of wing, a big tire, and parts of the landing gear. We began walking along the fence row, and we came across something thought to be part of a body. We just stood still and waited until the ambulances got there. It was just awful," Green told the newspaper.

The first emergency workers on the scene were Vaughn Zimmerman and his crew from the Walkersville Rescue Company. They had received a call about a plane crash. Without an exact location yet known, they simply sped in the direction of the black smoke north of town, near Devilbiss Road.

Zimmerman had no idea what type of aircraft had gone

down or what the emergency crews would find. "Once we climbed the fence and went into the field, we had barley up to our knees," Zimmerman recalled. "Then we started finding bodies."

Decades after a military plane slammed into a Walkersville farm field, killing all 21 on board, the vivid, sometimes-graphic memories remain for those on the ground that day.

Rescue crews begin work at the crash site debris field. Photo courtesy of Vaughn Zimmerman.

Crash site

The plane was callsign AGAR 23, an U.S. Air Force EC-135N surveillance jet—a model often described as a Boeing 707 for the military. It took off from Wright-Patterson Air Force Base near Dayton, Ohio, at 10:05 a.m. on a training mission. Twenty-one people, including the two pilots' wives, were on board.

Forty-five minutes after takeoff, the plane was traveling eastward above Frederick County when it dropped off radar as it suddenly rolled and nosedived from 30,000 feet. The plane plunged toward the ground at 400 mph for 90 seconds and began breaking up at about 5,000 feet. It exploded shortly before crashing into the Walkersville field.

"The crew did not have time to relay anything or might have been incapacitated due to a number of things causing the breakup of the airplane very rapidly," John Galipault, president of the Aviation Safety Institute, said at the time.

John Luntz was driving a locomotive engine along the tracks when he heard an explosion. He leaned out of the cab to see what had happened, but he couldn't see anything because of the fog and rain. Then he heard a second explosion. A few moments later, The Gettysburg Times reported he came across debris and bodies on the track.

"The smell of the burning bodies was terrible. I was afraid to walk, as the rye, I think that what it was in the field, was about waist high and I didn't know what I might find," Paul Green Jr. told The (Frederick) News.

Chip Jewell, now retired as director of the Frederick County Division of Fire & Rescue Services, was a young fireman on the scene at the time. He recalled seeing the 10-by-10 nose cone from the plane, which fell in front of the locomotive.

Zimmerman directed the arriving crews, established their priorities, and tried to determine what the situation was. Brush units from Walkersville and Libertytown arrived and went to work, getting the small fires under control. Other fire and rescue units arrived to help. "Many of them left when it was obvious they weren't needed to put out fires or rescue anyone," Jewell said.

There was talk that the plane was military, but there had been no confirmation and no one could tell from the debris. "The plane had nearly disintegrated in flight, scattering, and debris was spread over a few acres," Jewell recalled. He rode with the Woodsboro Rescue Squad that day. "It floored me that something that big could crash and there wasn't much there."

He recalled an eerie scene. "It was a foggy, misty day, and there was little noise. Small fires were burning here and there, but there was no huge fireball of wreckage. The area smelled of burning fuel."

Debris at the Walkersville crash site. Photo courtesy of Vaughn Zimmerman.

When it became obvious there were no survivors, a search team was put together to mark where all the debris and human remains were. As people walked in a line, they would raise their hands and someone would come over with a wooden stake to mark the spot.

"It was pretty evident once we were in the field that we weren't going to find nothing but small pieces." Zimmerman said.

Military presence

When Zimmerman returned home the day of the crash and saw pictures of the Air Force plane on the television, he couldn't believe that a plane that size was the same aircraft that crashed into the field because of the lack of debris.

One exception was the cockpit, which was later found buried 30 feet in the ground in a crater. The military brought it a backhoe from Fort Detrick to recover the cabin. Five bodies were found inside.

By 1 p.m. on the day of the crash, volunteers had tagged the remains of 13 victims. As bodies were found, Zimmerman made sure they were covered. Forty years later, he is still proud: "We were able to give these people their dignity back."

He likened the scene to a bad automobile accident, but much worse given the number of victims. It would take two days before all the bodies were found and transported to Washington, D.C., for autopsies.

Representatives from the Department of Defense arrived around 1:30 p.m. to take over the scene. The Cumberland News reported that Maryland State Police confiscated the film of photographers from The Frederick Post and The (Hagerstown) Daily Mail. The police said they were acting on behalf of the Air Force.

Early news reports, refuted by the military, said the plane had been carrying classified documents when it went down. "Papers from the plane were strewn over the area, and state police worked to retrieve the documents, which were sodden from a light rain which feel throughout the day," the Associated Press reported. Jewell said any papers he saw looked like confetti, as if they had gone through a shredder.

With the military managing the scene, the civilian units were sent home. But a couple of days after the crash, military investigators visited the Walkersville ambulance station and asked if anyone had picked up a green oxygen bottle. "They were trying to piece the plane back together on the site and were looking for that piece for an unspecified reason," Zimmerman said.

Rescue crews begin work at the crash site debris field. Photo courtesy of Vaughn Zimmerman.

Two weeks later, investigators invited the ambulance crew back to the crash site to see the recovered parts of the plane before they were sent to Andrews Air Force Base in Camp Springs. "I was shocked they could put back together as much as they had," Zimmerman said. "And they were still looking for the green bottle. They seemed very concerned about it."

Investigators were so concerned that they visited the ambulance station once more, again asking about the bottle—and again, nothing. The bottle was eventually found months later by a farmer plowing his field.

Investigation

In June 1981, Air Force investigators said a malfunction of the flight control system while on autopilot caused the nosedive. Gen. Peter W. Odgers said, "We think that the autopilot possibly drove the trim system to a more nose-down position than would have been normal for that type of flight, and having recognized that, it was driven further for some unknown reason."

The rapid nosedive created two other complications for the crew: Anyone not strapped into a seat would have experienced zero-gravity conditions and the primary source of electrical power failed. Amid those obstacles, the pilot, Maj. Joseph C. Emilio, had just 8 to 10 seconds to pull the plane's nose up.

"The one thing we don't understand, nor can we simulate, is the confusion [in the cabin] or what could have inhibited [Emilio] from taking more aggressive action to try to raise the nose. I think we can say the pilot made every attempt to recover the aircraft," Odgers said at the time.

The explosion near the ground was caused by vapors from jet fuel that seeped from the bladder-like tanks in the belly of the aircraft, according to Odgers.

Although that remains the official explanation, Time Magazine and The Washington Post published stories in 1995, claiming that the two pilots' wives had climbed into the pilot and co-pilot seats and one had taken control of the plane before the crash. This was based on classified reports and the fact that Peggy Emilio's body had been found strapped into the co-pilot's seat.

The Air Force had acknowledged Peggy Emilio was in the left co-pilot's seat when the accident report was released, but the report also said she did not contribute to the accident. The official cause of the accident did not change, but shortly after the crash, the Air Force canceled the program that allowed spouses on the plane to observe a mission.

Jewell still thinks about that day and its aftermath, with an epilogue. While he credits the military and volunteers with a thorough search of the crash site, he doubts they found everything. "My guess is you could still find stuff out there," he said.

Gone Fishin'

History is obscure on how goldfish first came to the United States. The first recorded shipment was in 1878, but the specially bred Oriental fish were swimming in the American ponds and streams before then. Some records indicate it may have been long before then.

One thing is certain. Once goldfish were in the United States, they found Frederick County, Maryland, to their liking. During the first half of the 20th century, Frederick County produced 80 percent of the goldfish in the country, according to The (Frederick) News.

While farmers can raise many types of fish, goldfish, unlike other types of livestock and crops, are not generally considered food. You can eat beef, get eggs from chicken and wear cotton. You can even eat other types of farm-raised fish like trout and catfish.

But what do you do with a goldfish?

It is an ornamental fish, a pet.

The Chinese first bred goldfish for their color. As far back as 900 A.D., the Chinese noticed the crucian carp, a small, predominantly dark fish, sometimes had yellow on its fins and the ventral part of its body.

"In China at that time, anything that was yellow in color was considered valuable by the nobility, because gold is yellow. So the nobles kept all these yellow fish themselves, showing them off in decorative pools and elaborate containers," wrote Ernest Tresselt in his memoirs, *Autobiography of a Goldfish Farmer.* Tresselt was raised on a goldfish farm, Hunting Creek Fisheries in Thurmont, Md. He also ran it after his father retired in 1962.

As the gold-colored carp bred with each other, the color passed on from generation to generation. The selective breeding also led to different varieties with unusual shapes, like the bubble-eye goldfish whose eyes are nearly as big as its body and bulge out to the sides of its head. A variety called the "telescope" has huge eyeballs.

One of the many varieties of goldfish raised at Hunting Creek Fisheries. Photo courtesy of Ernest Tresselt.

Around the 16th century, the Japanese began cultivating goldfish. They developed many new types and colors to include yellow-gold, red-gold, red, white and black.

When goldfish came to America is uncertain, but one research paper in the journal, *Fisheries,* noted: "The only reasonably well-supported record of a foreign fish introduced into this country prior to 1850 is of goldfish." The article has 1842 as the earliest date and that in 1879 "goldfish could be found in great number in the Hudson River of New York; most specimens were of drab wild colors, but a few could be found that were 'white, red, and all intermediate conditions.'" Goldfish in 1879 were also sold in New York markets as a food fish, according to National Geographic.

P.T. Barnum took credit for imported goldfish in 1850, though no evidence supported this and another unsupported account said a pet store in New York was selling goldfish as pets in 1865.

Hugo Mulertt in his 1883 book, *The Goldfish and its culture*, wrote that goldfish have been introduced into Ohio in the early 1840s. Part of his reasoning was that goldfish could be found in many streams in that area.

In 1878, Rear Admiral Daniel Ammens brought a shipment of these beautiful goldfish from Japan to the United States Commission on Fisheries. This is the first recorded entrance of goldfish into the United States.

It is these goldfish that most likely took hold in Frederick County.

Because of the limited number of native freshwater fish in the United States, the United States Commission of Fisheries (created in 1871) and the Maryland Commission of Fish and Fisheries (created in 1874) introduced European carp into American waters as a supplementary food source for farmers.

Ponds were created for the carp on the grounds of the Washington Monument in Washington, D.C. and Druid Hill Park in Baltimore. For a shipping fee of two dollars per can, the government would ship carp by rail car and truck all over the country. Once delivered, the empty cans were returned to Washington and Baltimore.

The fish cans were circular metal containers, similar to

milk cans, though somewhat squatter. They weighed about 75 pounds when filled with fish and water. The lids were perforated with holes. Ice was placed into a holder on the lid so that it would melt gradually in hot weather, drip into the fish water and keep the fish cool. Each can could hold between 250 and 1,000 small goldfish.

One of the many goldfish ponds at Hunting Creek Fisheries from the 1960s. Photo courtesy of Ernest Tresselt.

Once Ammens' goldfish came to the United States, they were kept in ponds near the carp. The goldfish produced so many offspring that they were sold along with the carp to anyone interested in them.

"Since Frederick County, especially the Thurmont area, was settled by Germans who ate a lot of fish, the fish in the area were used up by this time. German families were raised on carp and so many of them purchased carp from the government," said Tresselt.

Albert Powell, former superintendent of Maryland fish

hatcheries, does not mention goldfish in his manuscript, "Historical Information of Maryland's Commission of Fish and Fisheries with some notes on Game." This is because goldfish are not considered a game fish, which is the responsibility of the Commission of Fish and Fisheries. Because goldfish are ornamental fish and pets, they are tracked as a crop. Many reports, in fact, call goldfish a crop that was "harvested" in the fall.

A 1921 The Catoctin Clarion article describes a goldfish harvest this way:

> "A sluice gate was slightly raised; at the end of the sluice a large wire basket encloses everything that comes through and a small dip net transfers the fish to buckets, whence they are taken to the sorting room. Here they are emptied about a quart at a time on a table with a sloping galvanized iron top, and as they slide by, four men separate the gold fish from the uncolored gold fish, the tadpoles, crabs, frogs, pond bass, and various other pond inhabitants. The gold fish are put into large floats and afterwards, by the same process above are sorted into their different sizes."

Powell does, however, note in his manuscript that some of the fish introduced in the Druid Hill Park fish ponds were golden, such as golden tench and orphes. They were among the fish that the fish commissioners began to ship to the public in 1878.

"That's how goldfish found its way to the Maryland countryside, on the tails of edible carp. It is easy to speculate that one or more farms in Frederick County got goldfish along with their carp during the period when the carp culture in farm fish ponds was advocated as a supplementary food supply," wrote Tresselt.

The first record of a goldfish farmer in Frederick County is Charles J. Ramsburg. He was born and raised in Lewistown, but he attended college at Eaton and Burnett's Business College in Baltimore. He returned to the family farm after he graduated in 1884. Part of his farming operations was to raise goldfish. By the early 1900s, he was shipping about a million fish a year around the country, according to History of Frederick County.

Another pioneer in goldfish farming was Ernest R. Powell of Lewistown. "When he was twelve years old, he began breeding gold fish, and was so successful in his enterprise that he increased his output every year, and is now one of the largest dealers of gold fish in Frederick County," according to his biography in History of Frederick County. Powell would have been 12 years old in 1892.

More farmers began entering the business using existing farm ponds or new ponds dug by hand with shovels, wheelbarrows and horse-drawn scoops.

"In the early part of the century, I think people in the county, especially farmers, saw goldfish as a way of making extra money," Tresselt said.

He said the reason goldfish farming flourished in the county is unknown, "but it appears to be related to the availability of water on many farms because of the mountain streams and springs. The temperate climate, with its distinct seasonal changes, is ideal for the propagation of goldfish."

George Leicester Thomas, who founded Three Springs Fisheries in 1917, had his own ideas about why goldfish were successful in Frederick County. He said in interviews in The Frederick Post that the water in Frederick County was well-suited for goldfish, perhaps because of the mineral content. It gave the Frederick County the reputation for having the best-colored goldfish in the country.

Thomas' grandson, Charles, said in 1981 that the rich-colored goldfish came because the county farmers used good breeding stock, but he also notes they lived in nutrient-rich water from truckloads of manure dumped in the ponds.

"The manure has nutrients that fish thrive on and actually all they have to do is open their mouths in order to eat," said Charles Thomas.

George Thomas started his business as road side stand that sold vegetables and goldfish. This grew into Three Springs Fisheries in Buckeystown and is known today as Lilypons. Thomas owned a farm and grew vegetables, but he also raised goldfish as a hobby. He set up a roadside stand to sell his vegetables and display his goldfish.

Holding tanks for goldfish raised at Hunting Creek Fisheries. Photo courtesy of Ernest Tresselt.

"He had a keen eye for finding some type of venture where he might be successful," Charles Thomas said.

While customers may have bought his vegetables, they

showed more of an interest in his goldfish. By the end of World War II, Lilypons had become the world's largest producer of goldfish.

Hunting Creek Fisheries near Thurmont was started by Frederick Tresselt in 1923. Frederick Tresselt was a graduate of Cornell and had worked at the state trout hatchery in Hackettstown, New Jersey.

"In driving around the county with a friend in 1922, Dad was amazed to see all the goldfish ponds in the area," Tresselt said.

Other Frederick County goldfish farmers included George English, Frank Rice, Earl Rice, Maurice Albaugh, M.H. Hoke, Ross Firor, Sam Eaton, David and Adam Zentz, Walter Rice, Joseph Weller, Richard Kefauver and Martin Kefauver.

"Every farm that could had fish ponds," Tresselt said. "It was a cash crop for them."

Tresselt believes that Frederick County might not have the oldest goldfish farms in the country, but the county did have the most goldfish farmers. At the peak of goldfish farming in the county (the 1920s and 1930s), he estimates that as many as 30 or more farms were raising goldfish. The county had enough farmers that they organized as the Goldfish Breeders Association of Frederick County in 1920 to fight against the high cost of shipping.

The 1925 News-Post Yearbook and Almanac listed the county's production at 3.5 to 4 million goldfish on 400 to500 acres. Production in 1932 was 7 million goldfish on 500 to 600 acres.

The 1925 yearbook notes, "They (goldfish) are marketed at from $10 to $50 per thousand, value of yearly production being about $75,000."

In 1932, goldfish up to 2.5 inches long were sold for about $3.50 per 100 and retailed for five cents apiece and larger goldfish sold for about $7 per 100 and retailed for 10 cents apiece. By this time, most reports estimated Frederick County farmers had been raising goldfish for about 50 years and had brought $1.5 million into the county.

By 1931, the U.S. Commerce Department said the United States goldfish industry was a $945,000 business in the country and at that time 80 percent of that was coming into Frederick County.

Early goldfish farming was relatively simple. In the spring, farmers stocked their ponds with breeder goldfish. The goldfish reproduced, and the young grew through the summer and were harvested in the fall. The breeders were kept in the deepest ponds, since these ponds provided a good water supply over the winter.

In the fall, buyers would come driving trucks full of fish cans and buy the fish or farmers would ship the fish to the buyers. A single farmer would ship thousands of fish each day during the harvest. During the 1904 harvest season, goldfish farmer M.H. Hoke was shipping about 6,000 goldfish each day that he harvested from his ponds near Walkersville, The (Frederick) News reported.

Once the crop was harvested, the farmers would drain their ponds and dry them over the winter as a means of sterilizing them.

Feeding the fish was kept at a minimum. Generally, some form of ground grain, like wheat middlings or ground corn, was the food of choice. Treatments for parasites and diseases were marginal. As the ponds became older, there was an increase in parasites problem.

Another problem involved the weather. Ponds located on streams could flood, sending hundreds of fish and dollars into the stream.

Crayfish were also said to bore holes in the sides of man-made ponds, which could cause them to leak and eventually break. In 1904, one of Richard Kefauver's Middletown ponds broke, and it was estimated he lost about $700 in goldfish, The (Frederick) News reported.

Other natural problems included fish cranes, hawks, kingfishers and water snakes, all of which had a taste for goldfish.

"By 1920, Frederick County was producing 80 percent of the goldfish in the United States, and they were being shipped from Thurmont to all parts of the country," George Wireman wrote in his book *Thurmont: Gateway to the Mountains*.

His number is supported with information in The News-Post Year Book and Almanac. Throughout the 1930s and into the 1940s, the annual publications note that Frederick County had "more goldfish produced than in any part of the United States." Interestingly, the yearbooks list goldfish as "selected crops harvested" rather than "livestock on farms."

The fish raised in Frederick County were considered common goldfish. A 1914 The (Frederick) News noted:

"Few, if any, of the Japanese variety are raised. They are said to be too clumsy and awkward and an easy mark for preying birds. No coloring is necessary for the fish raised here, as is the case with those raised in some localities, where the fish have to be kept in shallow ponds in order to obtain their color."

By the late 1930s, competition from larger, more diversified, growers across the country reduced the demand from Frederick County farms. Tresselt said:

"Frederick County farmers raised the plain, common goldfish. By the 20s and early 30s, fancier varieties became available. It wasn't so easy for locals to keep up with the change. They weren't in a position to grow fancier varieties that were genetically difficult to breed and we lost some goldfish producers."

Tresselt said when he entered the family goldfish farming business, about 40 percent of each year's crop would not turn orange. They remained the dull, muddy color of wild goldfish.

"Those fish would be sold as bait fish. They were called Baltimore minnows," Tresselt said.

He said the county's goldfish breeders began more selective breeding of goldfish and the percentage of goldfish that turned the proper color dramatically increased and "Baltimore minnows" disappeared.

The use of modern science helped the goldfish farmers increase their harvests and profitability, which helped keep the county goldfish farmers competitive.

Other advances worked against county goldfish farmers. Advances in shipping techniques and the increased variety and quality of goldfish available from growers around the world gradually changed the goldfish market. The result was that farms producing only common goldfish seasonally could not compete. By the 1940s, only a few farms in Frederick County were still cultivating goldfish.

By the 1950s, fish could be shipped in plastic bags by air freight. The plastic made shipping costs cheaper, and the planes extended the distance the goldfish could be shipped. This increased the competition in the market, particularly from the countries in the Orient that had created goldfish.

"Everything changed," Tresselt said. "We have to supply fish year round. The competition made it unprofitable for most farmers and they went out of business."

Charles Thomas said that with air transportation, areas that usually weren't thought of as places for goldfish farming, such as Arkansas, became competitive or even better locations than Frederick.

Harvesting goldfish at Hunting Creek Fisheries. Photo courtesy of Ernest Tresselt.

"By going south, you had a longer growing season," said Charles Thomas. "In a place like Arkansas, instead of having only one crop each season, you could have two."

By 1980, Lilypons, once the world's largest producer of goldfish, had diversified so that it now specializes more in water garden supplies and plants than fish. Hunting Creek Fisheries and Eaton Fisheries also survived by diversifying their offerings into plants, game fish, and/or other types of ornamental fish, such as koi.

Today, you can still see fish ponds marked on a Frederick County maps, but not as many as there once were.

Lilypons has 265 acres and about 500 ponds, though

very few of them are devoted to goldfish. However, the business has grown into a multi-million business employing more than 50 people.

Hunting Creek Fisheries still has ponds in Thurmont and Lewistown. Eaton Fisheries still has its Lewistown ponds as well.

Other ponds are now lost to history:

- The Claybaugh fish ponds are now covered over by Mountain Gate Exxon and McDonald's in Thurmont.

- Along Moser Road across Hunting Creek from the Thurmont sewage treatment plant is where Ernest Powell and Maurice Albaugh used to have fish ponds.

- Ross Firor used to have his fish ponds east of the Maple Run Golf Course.

- The ponds on William Powell's Arrowhead Farms on Appels Church Road north of Thurmont were adjacent to Owens Creek and have been turned into pasture.

- Frank Rice's goldfish ponds south of Thurmont alongside Route 15 have been filled in and turned back to pasture.

Frederick County's no longer the biggest producer of goldfish in the country, but there are still fish ponds out there and if you stop and watch, you may see a flash of gold.

Triassic Park

T wo-hundred-and-twenty-million years ago, give or take a few million years, Frederick County (and, in fact, all of central Maryland) was part of a vast lake and mud flat that stretched from North Carolina to Connecticut. The Catoctin Mountains were not the mere hills they are today, but an enormous range towering as high as the Himalayas. A lake, known as the Lockatong, sat in the middle of Pangaea, an immense, C-shaped supercontinent.

Because of Pangaea's massive size, most of the inland areas were very dry. Lake Lockatong was one of the exceptions, though it could be more mud than water at times. Pangaea eventually broke apart, and the pieces spread to become the continents we know today.

It was a time of drastic climate change at the dawning of the Age of Dinosaurs. The lake began to dry and, as it did, some of its fish and other creatures found themselves trapped in small pools of water. When those pools evaporated, the critters died in the mud.

Small animals moved across the mud flats seeking water. Behind them, their prints remained, baked into permanence by the heat of the sun.

Years passed. Eons elapsed. The land changed. It cooled. Different types of vegetation arose. The mountains shrank due to eons of erosion. Man appeared.

John and Linda Ballenger own a 145-acre farm in Rocky Ridge that has been yielding its prehistoric secrets to researchers, simply because Linda thought to ask.

162

In 1994, John Edwards, with the Maryland Geological Survey, came to her door wanting to take some samples of the ground on the Ballenger Farm. "I jokingly said, 'If you find any dinosaur tracks, let me know,'" Linda recalled.

She went out to run errands, but when she returned, she found a note reading, in part, "These marks on the rock surface may be nothing at all, but it is possible that they may be the tracks of some small lizard-size or mouse-size animal. Possibly a small dinosaur?"

Linda walked out into the fields where she had seen Edwards go and searched for the pieces of white paper he had left behind to mark what he thought might be tracks. When she found them, she wasn't sure what she was looking at, either.

And she wouldn't be sure for another 10 years. That's when she read a newspaper article in The Emmitsburg Dispatch about a quarry at the north end of Emmitsburg, where dinosaur fossils had been found. She contacted the article's author, Richard D.L. Fulton, and told him that her farm might also have dinosaur tracks.

Fulton, who was also a published lay-professional paleontologist, visited the farm and confirmed Linda's find. He then asked permission to begin studying the farm for other evidence of its prehistoric past. Since 2004, his search has yielded thousands of reptile tracks, skin impressions and bones, millipede and insect tracts, plant fossils, and fossil freshwater shrimp and fish.

"Most Eastern Triassic Age formations are void of fossils because the surface was too dry to hold impressions," Fulton said.

This is because during the Triassic Age (248 to 208 million years ago), Pangaea was so expansive—imagine all the world's land pushed together—that water picked up from the oceans never made it into the center of the continent as rain.

"This particular section of Triassic has a wet period that

we're looking at," said Fulton. "It was practically dead-center in the middle of the supercontinent, and it allows us to see life as it struggled in some serious climactic extremes."

Paul Olsen of Columbia University suggested that the Ballengers' farm is probably the lowest known area of Lake Lockatong.

One fossil found there was a nicely preserved imprint of a fish about four inches long. The fins, teeth, and scales can all be seen. According to Olsen, it represents the oldest dinosaur-age fish found to date east of the Mississippi River. Even more remarkable, the head of a second smaller fish appears to be jutting out of the head area of the four-inch fish, suggesting it may have been in the process of being eaten by the larger one.

Since the discovery of this fish slab, the remains of several other fish have been found, including the scales of a coelacanth (pronounced "SEE-la-kanth"). The prehistoric fish predates the dinosaurs by millions of years and was thought to have gone extinct until researchers discovered living ones in the Indian Ocean. Adults can grow to be 180 centimeters long and weigh more than 200 pounds. Each fish has a distinctive pattern of white blotches. Living, the coelacanth is generally dark blue. It turns gray or brown upon death.

Fulton and Olsen discovered a layer of shale in the lake bottom sequence containing the actual preserved bones of reptiles, which may have belonged to a lake-dwelling reptile. Robert Weems of the U.S. Geological Survey also discovered a footprint at the site.

Weems is a believer in the value of the site and visited it many times to examine what Fulton found and to dig some himself.

In March 2007, Weems brought colleague Heinz Kozur, a German researcher living in Hungary, to the site. After examining some of the fossils, Kozur spoke for a few minutes with

Weems. He then sat on what had once been mud flats and chipped away at large pieces of rock. He placed a jeweler's eyepiece to his face and examined the surface.

His conclusion? The fossils Fulton found are indeed pre-historic, but they were prehistoric when the big dinosaurs of the Jurassic and Cretaceous periods roamed the earth, too. One of Fulton's finds—the one Kozur was most interested in—was a tiny prehistoric shrimp called Cacostrian (or freshwater clam shrimp) that made a faint half-moon impression in the mud.

"Heinz has been working on these little critters in Germany," Weems said. "We've compared his finds to what we've found here and, for the most part, they seem to match up pretty good."

While the fish and lizard tracks Fulton found are interesting, a number of the clam-shrimp fossils actually appear to be a new species.

"The tracks and the fish are the icing on the cake," Weems said.

This one-of-a-kind discovery came down to the hard work of carefully opening up layers of earth and examining the pieces to see what might be a fossil and what might be just an odd twist of rock.

"You just have to open up the right layers," Fulton said. "I would not be surprised to find three to four different types of fish showing up with the time slices."

As far as being able to tell a fossil scale from a crack, Fulton said, "You learn to lock on patterns. You eventually know the rock so well that even a small, minute pattern change will stand out to the trained eye."

On the day Fulton found the fossil of a coelacanth scale, "The layer of rock where this was found is literally like a photograph of what happened that week," he said, or, pointing to a layer of fossil raindrop impressions, "that day 220 million years ago."

Another find on the Frederick County farm was the footprints of two types of a reptile resembling dicynodonts, one a mouse-size species and the other a larger animal about the size of a cat. Both were two-tusked herbivores, but more importantly, these animals were the last of a group of reptiles that gave rise to mammals and show traits of both reptiles and mammals. Fulton hopes eventually to find evidence of larger carnivores that would have fed on these small reptiles.

"Almost everything coming off this site is new science because so little is known," he said. "They are all firsts in Maryland."

The farm has also yielded some other unique finds: spear points left by Indians traveling on the old game trails thousands of years ago; government-issued nails from when Civil War cavalries camped on the land; limestone cobble in the creek from a forgotten ford.

While all these are interesting, it was the fossils that most fascinate Fulton and compelled him to continue chipping away at the earth.

"We were just speaking," Kozur said of a conversation he had with Weems. "We'll have to name some of these new species after him."

Welcome to Bird Land

I n November 1973, flocks of blackbirds, grackles, cowbirds, and starlings discovered the 60-acre white pine forest owned by Edgar Emrich of Graceham. Emrich had no trouble sharing his trees with the birds. There were thousands of trees that he had originally planned to sell as Christmas trees when he had planted them in 1957. He hadn't, and the tree farm had turned into a forest.

"I remember we'd go outside and make a game of trying to dodge the droppings," Mrs. Austin Young told The New York Times. "Of course, there were only thousands of them then."

As the months passed, more and more birds decided to call Graceham home, and by March 1974, an estimated 10 million birds had migrated there and Graceham was becoming known as Bird Land.

"Their problem apparently stems from a quirk in the migratory patterns of the birds. They flew south from their warmer-weather homes in New England and southern Canada, but something about Graceham suited them perfectly— Mr. Emrich's pine trees, or perhaps the rolling acres of fields nearby, and they settled in," The New York Times reported.

And the birds were causing problems. Dead birds abounded, droppings could be measured in inches, and the whole area had a foul odor. Residents had trouble sleeping because of all the chirping and shrieking from the birds at night. "Their flappingly thunderous comings and goings are frightening the children, unsettling the dogs and scaring the cows," according to The New York Times.

"Our dog Herman shakes when they fly by," Clare Myers told a reporter. "They go into his doghouse, chase him out and eat his food. We need help to stop this or otherwise we're going to turn into the world's biggest bird cage."

The birds ate the chicken and cattle feed before the animals it was meant for could get to it, and they even got into fights with cats and dogs.

The birds also affected the local flora and fauna. "Now, virtually every tree is dead or dying. The droppings, at least three inches thick after the last five months, have deadened the trees' roots," The (Abilene) Reporter noted.

Dr. Kenneth Crawford, a veterinarian with the Maryland Department of Health, said, "No robins, no pheasants, no rabbits—no wildlife of any kind is left in the grove. Those birds chased everything else away."

More importantly, the millions of birds represented a possible health hazard for the 400 residents of the town. The excessive dropping could cause histoplasmosis, a fungal disease that occurs in the soil where there is a large amount of bird or bat droppings.

Dr. Charles Spicknall, Frederick County chief public health officer "toured the bird roosting area at sunset just as the flock of an estimated several million blackbirds, starlings and grackles soared and swooped in from daytime feeding grounds up to fifty miles from the little hamlet of Graceham," The Frederick Post reported.

The town held a meeting in Graceham Moravian Church to discuss what to do about the birds. Poison was suggested, and Emrich even volunteered to dig a mass grave for the bodies.

Ornithologists said that birds would head north again during the spring and summer, but they also said they would probably return in the fall.

Graceham wasn't the only town experiencing problems with large numbers of birds. Hopkinsville, Kentucky; Albany, New York; Frankfort, Kentucky; and New York City were all having problems to one degree or another.

However, Graceham had another problem besides millions of birds, and that was dozens of media. Reporters, photographers, and the wire services were all driving to Graceham to report on the invasion of birds and their cars and trucks blocked the roads in the small town. Graceham was written about in newspapers all over the country.

A button created during the time millions of birds took over Graceham, Maryland. Photo courtesy of Thurmontimages.com.

A county meeting held on March 20 laid out a three-phase plan for getting rid of the birds. Phase 1 would use loud noises and explosive devices to scare the birds away. Phase 2 involved thinning out the pine grove to make it less attractive to the birds. Phase 3 was to develop a long-range program to ensure the birds didn't come back. Poison was once again mentioned, but only as a last resort.

Frederick County Commissioner Don Lewis said, "I'll not be a part to the mass killing of birds. We don't want to create a slaughter ground in Graceham."

Phase 1 was put into play the next evening. It began around 5:30 p.m. with shotgun blasts and explosive devices sounding off around the perimeter of the pine grove. Loud recordings of bird distress call and high-frequency sounds played in the grove. Around 7:30 p.m., it appeared that the birds were being discouraged and flying off elsewhere.

"Within 20 minutes, the tide shifted as the birds caught Crawford short of firepower on the southeastern perimeter and larger numbers of them began flying through the break," the Cumberland News reported.

Not to be discouraged, Phase 1 continued for five days. Crawford reported a 90 percent success rate, although residents were skeptical.

"We've won the battle but not the war," Crawford said. "We won't win the war until we eliminate the unbelievably dense forest that's there."

For Phase 2, every third row of trees in the pine grove was removed.

By the end of April the birds were gone, though whether it was the natural time to leave or they had been driven off by the noise was unknown.

Unfortunately, the bird returned again in October. Emrich said, "The birds are returning to my trees in increasingly large flocks. We don't have the big long streams we had last winter but they're increasing. They started coming back about two months ago and it looks like they're young birds who were born here last winter."

Luckily, they did not return in the millions, and fewer returned each season as the migratory patterns returned to normal.

An Unemployed Army Invades Frederick

T hey came as an army; not to conquer, but to have their voices heard.

They were a group of unemployed workers that formed in Massillon, Ohio, under the direction of Jacob Coxey. The official name of the group was the Commonweal of Christ, but most people referred to it as Coxey's Army. The group planned to march to Washington D.C. where Coxey would present his petition to Congress of his ideas for a national program of building and repairing roads that would also solve the national unemployment problem. The group started its march with much fanfare, leaving Massillon on Easter Sunday, March 25, 1894, and made its way slowly eastward. Their mission inspired other groups to set out for Washington, and by the end of April, more than 7,000 men were marching toward Washington from different locations across the country.

"Stories of pillaging, disorderly conduct, and even assaults by the band of men all served to alarm the local residents and spread fear and apprehension as to what the impending invasion would bring. Some news accounts were reporting that the army was infested with drunks, crooks, and toughs," Scott wrote. Harold Scott wrote in *Incredible, Strange, Unusual...*

While the actual situation was not that bad, the army did face deprivation and slow passage on the very roads they hoped to repair. Infighting over leadership of the group led to factions forming within it and even a mutiny as the two leaders vied for control of the army. Carl Browne, who had been appointed by Coxey to lead the group, was ousted from leadership and a group led by Unknown Smith took control for a short time. No one knew the man's name, and he refused to give it to reporters, so they called him "Unknown Smith." It took Coxey to restore Browne to his leadership role.

Jacob Coxey. Photo courtesy of Wikimedia Commons.

The group's primary route was along the National Road, and on April 24, after a month of travel, Coxey's Army prepared to invade Frederick County. The hundreds of men arrived at the Frederick County / Washington County line on the morning of April 24. They started down South Mountain and met Frederick County Sheriff Daniel Zimmerman and 30 mounted deputies at the county line around 9:30 a.m.

"The officers did not make any attempt to stop the army, but merely formed a line and preceded it toward the city of Frederick," John A. Grant wrote in *Coxey's 38-Day March Through the Alleghenies in Search of Economic Justice.*

Coxey's Army on the march. Photo courtesy of the Library of Congress.

Browne was traveling a half mile back from the front of the group when it reached the county line. When word reached him that the sheriff had been waiting for them, he rushed forward to deliver one of his "bombastic" speeches, only to find that the sheriff was leading them into Frederick.

Instead of criticizing the deputies, Browne said that "he felt much flattered by the fact that Frederick County had thought so much of the Commonweal as to send out such a handsome and well mounted reception committee," according to Grant.

However, the other members of the army weren't so happy to see the deputies. They cursed them and called them Pinkertons. Pinkertons were the private police and detectives that companies often hired for protection and strike breaking.

The army received a warm welcome in Frederick, which was unusual. For instance, they had passed through Middletown "without hurrah or harassment," according to Grant.

The Frederick drum corps met the army at the Frederick city line and led them into the town as residents stood on the sidewalks waving flags and cheering them.

Jacob Coxey met them at the Barbara Fritchie House. Though the group was named after Coxey, he rarely traveled with it. Instead, he traveled ahead and slept in rooms while the men who followed him were generally forced to sleep outside.

Coxey also had 35 new recruits and one old recruit who was rejoining the army with him. They called him Tooting John because he was a bugler.

The group then proceeded through Frederick. Coxey rode in his carriage, tipping his hat to people as they rode along to the baseball field.

There they set up Camp Lafayette and charged people 10 cents to see the camp. This is despite the fact they couldn't erect a circus tent that they typically used. It had an undisclosed problem, but the Salvation Army opened its doors and allowed the men to sleep in their building.

That evening, Coxey and Browne gave speeches to try to inspire the men in the army and the spectators. Roy Kirk, a reporter traveling with the army, read a telegram to the crowd from Henry Vincent in Chicago. Vincent had just come from a meeting of the Iron Molders Union and promised to have

1,000 men join Coxey in Washington on April 29. This brought a cheer from the audience. A group of women gave Browne a bouquet that he mounted on a 4-foot wooden shaft.

Coxey's Army on the march to Washington, DC. Photo courtesy of the Library of Congress.

"From that point onward, the reporters noted that a spirit of defiance seemed to pass through the Commonweal," Grant wrote.

Meanwhile, there were rumors floating through Camp Lafayette that 1,200 militia had been called up in Washington, D.C. to protect the city against the army.

That evening, it was decided to change the army's route. They had planned to travel further east toward Baltimore and then turn south at Ridgeville to go to Rockville. The route was altered to head directly to Rockville. This meant that Hyattstown and Gaithersburg would find themselves hosting the army. This did not set well with Gaithersburg, who started forming a minuteman group to protect property in the town.

On the morning of April 26, the men in the army ate breakfast, packed up, and formed into marching group. They headed out of Frederick at 8 a.m. once again led by the sheriff and his deputies. The Independent Fife and Drum Corps played them off with "Maryland, My Maryland."

From Frederick, the group was able to meet their deadline date to get to Washington, where thousands of people lined the streets to watch them march through the city. However, things still did not go smoothly.

"Before the marchers could present their petition, the police rushed them, and Coxey and the other leaders were arrested for trampling on the grass," Scott wrote.

Though the group failed that day, what they sought to achieve resonated with the public. Fifty years later, Coxey was finally able to read his speech from the Capitol steps. Grant also noted that many of Coxey's ideas became part of President Franklin Delano Roosevelt's New Deal Programs.

A Road by Any Other Name

Wishing people peace and goodwill can be a difficult thing to do.

In 1907, a Delaware-based real estate corporation bought property in Frederick City from R. Clinton Zimmerman and his wife. The company laid out a subdivision that the city adopted in September of that year.

One street in the subdivision was a short street between West College Terrace and Lindbergh Avenue, created to help traffic move through the development. When it came time to name the street, the company chose an Indian word for good fortune… swastika.

The word comes from the Sanskrit words *su,* meaning good, and *asti,* meaning to prevail. Together they mean well-being, prosperity, and good fortune. The word has been used in prayers from the Hindu scriptures. It has even been used as a girl's name in India.

"The emblem was a sign of well-being and long life, and was found everywhere, from the tombs of early Christians to the catacombs of Rome and the Lalibela Rock Churches, to the Cathedral of Cordoba," according to the BBC.

It has been found on Byzantine buildings, Buddhist inscriptions, Celtic monuments, and Greek coins.

"The motif appears to have first been used in Eurasia, as early as 7,000 years ago, perhaps representing the movement of the sun through the sky… as a symbol of wellbeing in ancient societies," according to the Holocaust Encyclopedia.

"The Russian Czarina Alexandria, Russia's very religious

last empress, frequently drew swastikas as a symbol of hope after the royal family was captured by the communists," according to The Frederick News-Post.

The intersection that was once known as Swastika Road in Frederick. Photo from the author's collection.

For decades, the street remained lightly traveled and unremarked upon. Then, unfortunately, Nazi Germany and the Third Reich adopted the swastika and its symbol of a cross with its legs bent at 90-degree angles as its symbol. It added a new meaning to the swastika that was diametrically opposed to its centuries-old meaning.

During and after the war, while the name raised some eyebrows, it didn't cause a controversy. Either people could separate the bad history from the good, or more likely, the name of a two-block-long road just wasn't a big deal for residents, even the city's Jewish community.

It wasn't until early 1960 that things changed. A group of teenagers in the city started leaving swastika symbols around town. It had nothing to do with Swastika Road, but apparently, people thought if they were going to have a problem with the symbols, then they should have a problem with the word and the street.

Mayor Jacob Ramsburg and the city council took up the issue after five city residents submitted a petition to change the name. The mayor and council agreed to change the name once they considered the suggested names to replace the offending name.

"As we ponder and discuss the question, I would urge our citizens with all the sincerity at my command that we permit no feeling of ill-will or ill-feeling, either expressed or implied, to enter our mind," Ramsburg said.

Meanwhile, property owners on or near Swastika Road submitted their own petition, calling the name change an "unwarranted and unnecessary expense." The petition noted, "If an enemy should happen to have used a 'Cross' or a 'Star of David,' we see no reason why we should then have to change the name of any street, lane or alley which bore a similar title. It seems that we have become quite excited just because some irresponsible youths, who seem to be badly in need of severe correction, have desecrated public places."

While this didn't stop the name change movement, it was not a high priority for the council. More than 60 new names for Swastika Road were suggested, and in the fall of 1961, more than a year and a half later, the mayor and council members selected Freedom Drive as the new name. Even though the name change was approved, the existing street signs remained in place until the following year. It wasn't until 1972, 11 years after the name change, that a new street sign was erected. It wasn't that the city hadn't tried to erect a new sign, but the local residents didn't want their street renamed.

In 1969, The Frederick Post reported, "Recently a new sign was erected but was removed hastily after irate citizens called for its removal."

Having the sign didn't stop people from calling the street by its original name. The Frederick News-Post reported in 1983, "And today, 11 years after the sign reinforced the change, the street is still commonly referred to as Swastika Road."

In particular, one person quoted in the article in the newspaper said police and fire personnel still referred to the street as Swastika Road. This lead to Frederick Police Chief Richard J. Ashton saying, "If you asked half the police force where Swastika Road was, they'd give you a blank stare."

City Planner Thomas Pauls told the newspaper that the name had been changed on all city maps. "As far as the city is concerned, it's called Freedom Drive."

The new interest in 1983 came as the city vacated ownership of land that was on a section of Swastika Road or Freedom Drive that was never built.

Today, Freedom Drive has now become of part of everyday life with people who pass it on their walks or drives never realizing that the city gave up peace and goodwill for freedom.

The Canal Snags on Point of Rocks

The Chesapeake and Ohio Canal was a construction and engineering challenge for its time. The canal's charter required that 100 operable miles be built within five years of the project's start on July 4, 1828. Benjamin Wright, who had overseen the construction of the Erie Canal, was chosen for the same job on the C&O Canal.

The canal construction involved more than just digging a trench across the level land and making it watertight. Boats traveling from Georgetown in the District of Columbia to Cumberland, Md., had to be lifted more than 600 feet on their westward journey. Rivers needed to be crossed and mountains gone over, around, or through.

The 184.5-mile-long C&O Canal was built in sections bid out to independent contractors. The laborers were mainly imported Irishman, who jumped at the chance to have a better life by immigrating to America. However, they quickly found that the work unsatisfying. They also faced discrimination, largely because of their religion. The work was hard, and the tools were picks, shovels, horses and black powder.

Even so, it was a chance to start over and better than what they had had in Ireland.

The canal hits its first major snag at Point of Rocks in Frederick County.

The canal was watered by dams built on the Potomac River. As the canal construction reached one of the barriers, water impounded by the dam was allowed to flow into the completed portion of the canal. The first dam was at Little Falls near where the canal groundbreaking ceremony with President John Quincy Adams had taken place. When the canal reached that point, that first section of the canal was placed into operation. It allowed the first five miles of the canal to be used.

In November 1830, construction reached the second dam at Seneca and opened the first 22 miles of the canal to navigations.

The third dam was near Harpers Ferry. Reaching this barrier would have opened up 62 miles of canal, but to get from Seneca to Harpers Ferry, the canal needed to pass through a narrow area of land called Point of Rocks, and that's where the forward progress of the canal stopped.

It was believed that the land there was wide enough for either the canal or the Baltimore and Ohio Railroad, and they both wanted that passage because it was the easiest way to get past Catoctin Mountain.

The B&O Railroad claimed the right of way through Point of Rocks. The C&O Canal Company thought it had the right of way by its own charter and the charter of the George Washington's Patowmack Company, which the C&O Canal had taken over.

The canal leadership had just assumed its rights were secure, but the railroad company was aggressively trying to secure its claim to the area, including getting waivers from landowners in the area, including Charles Carroll.

Carroll was a wealthy landowner and the last surviving signer of the Declaration of the United States. He was a supporter of the B&O Railroad and had been the guest of honor at the groundbreaking ceremony, which had taken place the same day as the C&O Canal groundbreaking. He fought the C&O Canal Company's right of way and encouraged other landowners to follow suit.

A view of Point of Rocks showing the C&O Canal and the B&O Railroad tunnel that passed through Catoctin Mountain. Photo courtesy of the Library of Congress.

The case went to court and stayed there for four years, during which time the C&O Canal could make no progress. Even if it had continued construction on the other side of Point of Rocks and reached the dam near Harpers Ferry, it would have been watering a canal to nowhere because the canal on the west side of the mountain would not have been able to connect with the canal on the east side of the mountain.

Meanwhile, unhindered by a need for a continuous flow of water, construction on the railroad continued.

The case was eventually decided in favor of the C&O Canal, but it left the company a financial wreck. The federal government, with a new administration, had grown disillusioned with the idea of the canal and stopped supporting it.

The canal company found new funding from the State of Maryland, but only after promising to build a canal extension to Baltimore if it was feasible.

While the court decided in favor of the canal, it did allow the railroad to build through Point of Rocks afterward if there was room. Although there was space for a single line through the area, when a second rail line was laid years later, a tunnel had to be built through Catoctin Mountain.

This meant that the canal and railroad were running side by side through Point of Rocks. This would happen at a couple other areas along the canal. These locations allowed for some venting of frustration between canallers and railroaders. The train engineers would show their animosity toward the canal by blowing their whistles when they passed canal boats in the hopes of startling the mules.

The Magnificent
Harney University

mmitsburg is known for being the home of Mount St.
Mary's University, but for a while, another nearby
university regularly appeared in the newspaper with
stories of great innovations in science and technology
that its learned professors developed.

That university? The esteemed Harney University.

Never heard of it? That's not surprising since despite all
the achievements credited to its faculty in The (Emmitsburg)
Weekly Chronicle, the university didn't exist...at least not as
an educational institution.

A group of residents met regularly at the Hotel Slagle and
came up with unusual stories that the newspaper published.

The faculty, as it was, consisted of Jacob Turner, Jerry
Overholser, Daniel Shorb, and Bill Snyder, who met regularly at the Slagle Hotel in Emmitsburg. The staff would have
also had to include Sterling Galt, editor of The (Emmitsburg)
Weekly Chronicle. Whether the group came up with the go-
ings-on at the university or it was something Galt did alone is
not known.

What is known is that the stories provided readers of the
Chronicle with a lot of smiles and laughs in the early 1900s.

"Uncle Bill's Column" seems to be the forerunner to
Harney University and seems very similar in the types of
achievements the university would later claim. In the column,
"Uncle Bill" answered such curious questions as: "Please

give in, in the Aztec language, a portion of Mrs. Roosevelt's remarks about Mr. Harriman" and "What noted fish are found in the Hongaloonbink River?"

In 1909, Dan Shorb, Bill Snider, Ed brown, and Nathan Hoke added to the Frederick County legend of the snallygaster by recounting their encounter with the beast. The men fought with it for hours, chasing it to Carroll County. It was described as having "ghost-like wings", bristles that stuck from its snout, and "its hide was the color of the downside of a catfish." It could also breathe fire.

A postcard view of the Slagle Hotel in Emmitsburg. Photo from the author's collection.

"Bill Snider says it sounded for all the world like Flat Run at high tide where the waters rush over the rocks at Whitmore's Wharf, only more so," the Chronicle reported. "The air was charged with some peculiar smell, rather loud too, for it wakened the man in the signal tower at Dry Bridge."

During 1910, a number of articles talked about an airship Dan Shorb built. It was 130 feet long and 16 feet wide and carried "two auto-magneto-bi-sparking generators, a cogless centripedal concussion plane and three wireless rudders," according to the Chronicle. It had an 87-horsepower engine fueled with horse mint oil. Its maiden voyage was to include dignitaries who would accompany the inventors "on this, the initial, and most likely, the final trip," according to the newspaper.

By 1912, Shorb was beginning to be called a doctor in the newspaper, a hint at what was to come. In May, the Chronicle ran a short piece about him proclaiming that he would not run for the presidential nomination of either political party.

The following piece ran in The (Emmitsburg) Weekly Chronicle in September 1912. Although it doesn't mention any of the typical members of the Harney University faculty, it definitely has the feel of one of their stories.

> "After many months of careful experimenting and the expenditure of $16,547 in real stage money, Drs. Herr Van Mueller and John E. Davidson, have perfected a flying apparatus, call by them the Gyro Scutoplane. It is propelled by an eight cylinder hexagonal engine using monkey feathers for fuel and is capable of attaining a speed of 85.6 miles a minute. A diagram and full particulars of this invention may be seen in the current issue of the Pallbearer's Review. Decorations have been given to the scientists and each has received a medal of the Order of the Plush Ladle, conferred by the Sultan of Slush."

By this time, Harney University had already started being mentioned in the pages of the newspaper, and a legend was born.

Here are some of the fantastical achievements of Harney University and its faculty.

October 7, 1910: The Harney University football team

won a game against a team from Pigs Misery. The game was played on Musk Rat Field, which was a gift to the university from Dan Shorb. Shorb was listed as a former professor of "Propaeduetics and a John Glass lecturer on the Theory of Aviation." The newspaper reported that 11,000 people attended the game and seven different bands played between quarters. One player named Murky Suds made a daring play. "This professional in a daring dash of 90 years with eighteen men on his neck, dislocated the goal post and tore away the gunwale and three hatchways on the port side of his physiognomy," according to The (Emmitsburg) Weekly Chronicle.

A drawing of Harney University that appeared in the Emmitsburg Chronicle.

March 15, 1912: Roald Amundsen was the first person to reach the South Pole. The (Emmitsburg) Weekly Chronicle disputed his claim, saying that Dr. John Glass and Dr. Bill Snyder of Harney University had found the pole two years earlier at 3 a.m., "brought it back to Harney, and preserved it in alcohol." The paper went on the further note, "Dr. Glass is not even willing to concede that Amundsen got to the farthest point south unless he is able to produce the lawn mower which Dr. Snider left on the front lawn under the cherry tree near the house which they lived while in those southern parts."

November 15, 1912: Dr. Dan Shorb received the election returns using an intricate machine so that "long before the telegraph instruments of the county had ticked the news, Prof. Bushman, who had his airship anchored on the prairie dog house nearby, was on his way to Emmitsburg with bushel baskets filled with the correct information," according to the Chronicle. He also claimed not to need his wireless device to get the returns from Thurmont, Harney, and Jimtown. His eyesight was so good, "He simply looked over the shoulders of the clerks, from his private office at Pigs Misery, and wrote down the results. Some slight difficulty was experience in reading the tally sheet at Poplar Ridge, owing, the doctor said, to a bad wick in one of the lamps at that place," the Chronicle reported.

November 29, 1912: President Woodrow Wilson was planning on appointing Dr. John Glass and Professor Dan Shorb of Harney University to help revise the tariff code on codfish balls. "Clarence Buckingham, brother of the Duke of Buckingham, will also revise the tariff on dill pickles. In an unrelated note, Col. Stonebottle, one of the most prominent citizens of Emmitsburg, painted his overalls on Saturday," the Chronicle reported.

December 13, 1912: The Harney University faculty held a

pinochle tournament competing for a trophy. It had been a dill pickle in 1911. "The trophy this year will be a loving cup filled with spinach, presented for this event by the Young Lady Society for the Prevention of the Use of the Denatured Alcohol and Strawberry Shortcake," according to the Chronicle.

January 24, 1913: The Khedive of Egypt sent Dr. Dan Shorb a wireless message that consisted of four lines of gibberish made up of letters (some upside down) mixed with numbers (including fractions) a few odd characters. Translated, the message was supposedly talking about how the parcel post system in Egypt was so successful and required so many camels that the manufacturing of camel-hair brushes, camel hair shawls, and "camelopards" had ceased.

July 25, 1913: Harney University now had a War College, which the federal government was consulting over how to handle tensions with Mexico. The recommendation of the War College was that seven airplanes loaded with molasses be sent to the border along with troops from Zora, Four Points, and Poplar Ridge who would be armed with 800,000 rounds of Limburger bullets.

According to The (Emmitsburg) Weekly Chronicle, the plan was simple. "The molasses will be released from the aero-planes, about 100 tons from each machine. This will have the same effect on the enemy as tangle-foot flypaper has on flies. When the opposing forces are rendered incapable of marching or standing erect, Limburger bullets will be discharged at them at a rate of 10,000 a second. Death will be instantaneous due to the smell of the cheese. An important feature of this mode of warfare is that death will be so horrible that no further recruiting will be possible–no one will enlist in the Mexican army."

August 8, 1913: Jacob Turner was appointed the chair of snakeology at the University of Harney. He wanted to offer a correspondence course in snake charming. "The professor now has 28 snakes of different varieties fully trained and he says he has no difficulty in making them do anything he asked. In the collection, there are two copperheads which he has taught to dance the tango and a black snake taught to walk the slack wire blindfolded," the Chronicle reported.

September 12, 1913: Twenty-seven men, under the direction of Dr. Jerry Overholser and Dr. Daniel Shorb from the University of Harney, built an airship underwater. "The main feature of the engine, which is of the complex eccentric type, is the simplicity of the duplicidentate. The meta centre articulates with the friction real and top buttons on the warping chock. This flutes the suction pipe in such a manner as to lap joint the back gear. The lubricator, connecting with a center balance spring, throws the pinch cock under the carburetor, at the same time opening the muffler cutout near the nephoscope. This feeds the silo juice through the bunghole and sparks the fifth wheel near the gunwale. The cloud anchor, which is regulated by a heliograph, is so adjusted on the pinochle deck that its releases automatically from the whiffletree, making it possible to stop and remain stationary by putting on the reverse clutch while going at the rate of 184 knots a second."

They planned to take the ship on a test flight from the Popular Ridge standpipe to the Eiffel Tower, stopping for lunch at the Sandwich Islands.

September 27, 1913: Dr. John Glass of Harney University came out against the Federal Reserve, issuing smaller bank notes. Instead, he had a formula using rubber and yeast that he wanted currency printed on. He told The (Emmitsburg) Weekly Chronicle, "Expandable bills will allow local residents to stretch their dollars further, allowing more to be bought with each bill."

October 15, 1915: James Arnold and Howard Harbaugh went hunting with Shorb and brought back a Gnukokukua

Hen, three Aviskovis Hawks, and a Night Heron, which were supposedly displayed in the Chronicle's front window.

October 8, 1915: Daniel Shorb of the "Board of Strategy, of Harney University" invented a rapid-fire noodle soup gun for the French Government. The gun fired noodles to entangle the legs of enemies and feed them when they were your prisoner. The French ordered 5 million of them and awarded Shorb the Order of the Imperial Soup Ladle and granted him a lifetime pension of 450,000 francs annually. He was also working on a macaroni tent that would both feed and shelter prisoners.

December 12, 1918: George Sanders sued the Emmitsburg Motor Car Company because the company sold a car to Rebecca Shorb, who then proceeded to get into an accident with Sander's horse-drawn wagon. The Chronicle reported, "Mr. Sanders, citing evidence recently published by the University of Harney that women's brains did not have sufficient capacity to master the art of driving, feels that the Emmitsburg Motor Car Company should not have sold Miss Shorb the car. 'By selling a car to a woman,' Mr. Sanders said, 'they have endangered all hard working men who have to use the roads to make a living, and thus are liable for any damage they produce. Women should stick to their proper roles— namely cooking, cleaning and taking care of youngins, and leave complex tasks that require thinking to men.'"

Acknowledgements

I wanted to thank all of those people who helped me put the *Secrets of Frederick County* together. The longer I work as a writer, the more I realize that while one person may publish a book, the effort is much richer when others assist.

I've been writing articles about the history of this region for nearly two decades. I've been doing the Secrets books for eight years. *Secrets of Garrett County* was the first book in the series. *Secrets of Frederick County* is No. 9. I wrote it way back in 2017, and I have a list of topics for future Secrets books that I will never be able to complete, particularly when you consider all the other book ideas I have.

One great local resource for finding the stories in this book was digitized editions of the county newspapers found on various websites. I was also helped by people like Thurmont Mayor John Kinnaird and Mary Mannix, head of the Maryland Room in the C. Burr Artz Library in Frederick, Md. They shared their knowledge and resources to help me along.

Since many of the stories in the Secrets books have appeared in newspapers and magazines, I get e-mails and phone calls from readers with new ideas and additional information that I try to incorporate into these book versions of the stories.

Finally, I'd like to thank Grace Eyler with E Plus in Emmitsburg, Md., for not only creating another great-looking cover but also being able to create the template for the Secrets series.

I have probably missed someone who I'll remember after

this book goes to print. If so, it's not because I didn't appreciate your input. I sometimes get confused juggling all the projects that I do. If I did leave you out, mention it to me.

Meanwhile, I'm off to work on my next project.

James Rada, Jr.
March 1, 2024

About the Author

J ames Rada, Jr. is an Amazon.com bestselling author of historical fiction and non-fiction history. They include the popular books *Strike the Fuse, Canawlers,* and *Battlefield Angels: The Daughters of Charity Work as Civil War Nurses.*

He lives in Gettysburg, Pa., where he works as a freelance writer. James has received numerous awards from the Maryland-Delaware-DC Press Association, Associated Press, Maryland State Teachers Association, Society of Professional Journalists, and Community Newspaper Holdings, Inc. for his newspaper writing.

If you would like to be kept up to date on new books being published by James or ask him questions, he can be reached by e-mail at *jimrada@yahoo.com.*

To see James' other books or to order copies on-line, go to *www.jamesrada.com.*

PLEASE LEAVE A REVIEW
If you enjoyed this book, please help other readers find it. Reviews help authors get more exposure for their books. Please take a few minutes to review this book at *Goodreads.com.* Thank you, and if you sign up for his mailing list at *jamesrada.com*, you can get FREE ebooks.

WANT TO KNOW MORE SECRETS?

Find out the little-known stories and hidden history of Maryland and Pennsylvania with the Secrets series from James Rada, Jr.

Available wherever books are sold.

.

www.ingramcontent.com/pod-product-compliance
Lightning Source LLC
Chambersburg PA
CBHW060809120626
46557CB00001B/142